Battle of the Books

———

The Great Pretender *(fiction)*
Delmore Schwartz: The Life of an American Poet

Battle of the Books

The Curriculum Debate in America

James Atlas

W. W. NORTON & COMPANY
New York   London

An earlier version of this book was published by Whittle Books as
part of The Larger Agenda Series. Reprinted by arrangement with
Whittle Communications, L.P.

The text of this book is composed in Caledonia.
Composition and manufacturing by the Haddon Craftsmen, Inc.

Library of Congress Cataloging-in-Publication Data
Atlas, James.
Battle of the books / by James Atlas.
p.   cm.
1. College students—United States—Books and reading.   2. Ethnic
groups—United States—Bibliography—Methodology.   3. Pluralism
(Social sciences)—Bibliography—Methodology.   4. Books and
reading—United States.   5. Education, Higher—United States.
I. Title.
Z1039.C65A74   1992
028.5′35—dc20   92–20032

ISBN 0–393–03413–5

W. W. Norton & Company, Inc.
500 Fifth Avenue, New York, N.Y. 10110
W. W. Norton & Company Ltd.
10 Coptic Street, London WC1A 1PU

1 2 3 4 5 6 7 8 9 0

Contents

"The disputants have admirably managed the dispute between them, have taken in the full strength of all that is to be said on both sides, and exhausted the substance of every argument *pro* and *con*. It is but to adjust the reasonings of both to the present quarrel, then to compare and apply the labours and fruits of each . . . and we shall find the conclusion fall plain and close upon us."

—Jonathan Swift,
"The Battle of the Books" (1704)

Foreword

When does an issue become an issue? Five years ago no one except professional educators paid much attention to what was happening in our universities and schools. Now it often seems as if no one can talk about anything else. The *New York Times Magazine* runs a cover story on California's textbook debate. *Time* runs a cover story on multiculturalism. *Newsweek* runs a cover story on the campus phenomenon of "p.c."—political correctness. *Illiberal Education: The Politics of Race and Sex on Campus,* by Dinesh D'Souza, hits the best-seller list. The *MacNeil/ Lehrer Newshour* devotes a week to exploring the issues raised by D'Souza's book. Even George Bush has weighed in, decrying p.c. as a threat to academic freedom in a commencement address at the University of Michigan. For a man who had never laid eyes on a supermarket price scanner to have noticed the crisis in American education is perhaps the clearest evidence that there is one.

Indeed, at first glance, there appear to be several crises, beginning with the curriculum debate that has flared up in the universities. Put simply: *Should there be books that are required reading, and what books should they be?* This apparently innocent question provokes others that are more charged: How are these books chosen? Is there such thing as a "canon," a core curriculum of works that represents, in the words of Matthew Arnold, "the best that is known and thought in the world"? If so, how is this canon determined? Do political and social interests figure in its composition? Are some books more universal than others? Does "opening the canon"—including works of other peoples and cultures that have been largely ignored, or *marginalized*—promote tolerance and widen our horizons, or does it produce an educational free-for-all, a "Balkanization of culture," in which no one learns anything? What does it mean to be educated in America today?

This primary issue, so easy to state when it was first raised and so exceedingly complex the more closely it's examined, quickly escalated into a debate over multiculturalism. Again, put simply: *Has the*

United States become too diverse a society to embrace one idea of itself? Is the notion of a "collective culture" obsolete, or is it necessary to our survival as a nation? Does the widening of the curriculum to recognize the cultural achievements of such disenfranchised constituencies as women, blacks, Hispanics, and Native Americans confirm our democratic charter, or does it threaten to promote—in Arthur M. Schlesinger, Jr.'s resonant phrase—"the disuniting of America"? Is multiculturalism a harbinger of anarchy?

These questions are by no means theoretical. The emergence of the curriculum debate has provoked a serious power struggle among students and faculty, government officials and university administrators, even parents. Who gets to decide what books—even what languages—are taught in our schools? Is the canon an instrument of oppression—"the *property* of a small and powerful caste that is linguistically and ethnically unified," to quote Stanford professor Mary Louise Pratt? Or is it potentially an instrument of liberation that will enable minorities to achieve self-esteem and—ultimately—political and economic power? Whose canon is it, anyway?

The turf that's being struggled over now covers a lot more than reading lists. At issue are college admissions policies, the merits of affirmative action, the representation of minorities on college faculties, and the incidence of bias—both real and imagined—on campuses across the country. Dinesh D'Souza's book reported on a number of ominous developments that have since become shibboleths of "p.c."—regulations

against racial or sexual harassment; censorship of remarks that could be construed as derogatory toward
any group; seminars in tolerance. "An academic and
cultural revolution is under way at American universities," D'Souza contended. "It is revising the rules by
which students are admitted to college, and by which
they pay for college. It is changing what students
learn in the classroom, and how they are taught." And
not just at the college level: the revolution that he
describes has spread to high schools, junior high
schools, grammar schools. Textbooks are being revised to reflect the new dogma of inclusion. Revision-
ist interpretations of history that seek to rectify a perceived imbalance in the treatment of minorities by
dwelling on their achievements have been widely
adopted. The politics of ethnic representation are as
common a feature of American public education now
as the pledge of allegiance and compulsory gym.

On first inspection, the antagonists in the battle
of the books seem easy to determine. The lines are
clearly drawn. On one side are the neo-conservatives,
holding the line on behalf of Western civilization and
its high cultural monuments, openly disdainful of ethnic minorities and other potentially unruly constituencies. Their official ally is the National Association of
Scholars, which has denounced "the political agenda"
of "our new academic mandarins" (I'm quoting Hilton Kramer, editor of the neo-conservative *New Criterion*). On the other side is the academic left, a
"Rainbow Coalition of feminists, deconstructionists,
Althusserians, Foucauldians, people working in ethnic
or gay studies, etc."—as the black literary scholar

Henry Louis Gates, Jr., describes these new mandarins—that stands in opposition to the "patriarchal hegemony" of the "DWEMs," or Dead White European
Males. *Their* ally is Teachers for a Democratic Culture, which has denounced the National Association
of Scholars for "endangering education with a cam-
paign of harassment and misrepresentation." On one
side—to choose a representative example—is Diane
Ravitch, the assistant secretary of education, decrying
multiculturalism as a threat to the principle of "E
Pluribus Unum." On the other is Dr. Leonard Jeffries,
Jr., the notorious professor of African-American Studies at the City College of New York, provoking turmoil
on campus with his poisonous anti-Semitic theories.

But nothing is so simple—least of all in this debate. Consider the position of Richard Rorty, a distinguished philosopher and educator firmly identified (in
the minds of his opponents, anyway) with the academic left. In a notably balanced essay entitled "Two
Cheers for the Cultural Left," Rorty, who describes
himself as "a reformist, bourgeois, Dewey-style liberal," offers his views on a conference held in 1988 at
Duke University that received a great deal of attention in the media. Our society isn't repressive, Rorty
insists, but largely "reasonable." He's progressive, a
reformer, though wary of revolutions and "transfor-
mations"; he believes in teaching our children the
"standard" lore of American history as it used to be
taught, "the canonical narrative of origins"; he's more
concerned with making sure they're literate than with
their political correctness quotient. "You cannot make
a free individual out of an unsocialized child," as

Rorty succinctly puts it. Where does this place him on the ideological spectrum? To the left or to the right? For or against a core curriculum? Somewhere in between, is my guess. "This is a time of excitement in the humanities, and the rate of canon change is speeding up," Rorty concludes:

> Such changes seem to me all to the good, as long as they do not lead us to give up the very idea of a canon. There is, after all, a good pragmatic reason for overlap in reading lists across time and space: parents and children can communicate more easily if they have read some of the same books, as can, say, graduates of Amherst and of Miami-Dade Community College.

Stated in this plain-spoken, unpretentious way, with a minimum of polemical fervor and a willingness to acknowledge both the merits of tradition and the inevitability of change, the argument for a canon makes good sense.

I am neither a professional educator nor a policy analyst, neither a Marxist academic nor a neo-conservative. A critic and biographer by trade, I prefer narrative to theory. What are my credentials for writing about this issue? I have none, really: I studied literature in college, once taught a graduate seminar in American literature, and often visit college campuses. I read and write books. I have also written a good deal of literary journalism; I like to go out into the field and cover a story as it develops, allowing the lineaments of the narrative to emerge from my research. I have treated the curriculum debate like a story, notebook in hand, weighing the evidence on both sides and arriving at my own conclusions. I am aware that even to presume disinterestedness is against the rules at this late date: any reader of contemporary literary criticism knows by now that no text is free of ideology, that every statement carries within it the seeds of its own undoing. The very notion of objectivity has been thrown out of court. Let's say, then, that I've written this book in a spirit of curiosity, trying to give both sides of the story. Much of what has been published on the curriculum debate in America over the last few years has been tendentious and inflammatory. Journalists have over-simplified the issue, professors have resorted to academic jargon, politicians have entered the fray without having a clue as to what it's about. Barbara Herrnstein Smith, one of the most intrepid defenders of innovation in the college classroom, complains in her introduction to *The Politics of Liberal Education* that the press has badly misrepresented the whole debate, caricaturing complex arguments and inflaming the controversy with "a remarkable series of cross-citing and mutually puffing newspaper articles, magazine stories, and topical books, duly peppered with selective statistics, evocatively illustrated by menacing photos, and obviously produced by and for persons remote from the scenes of the alleged crimes."

Maybe so, but anyone who tries to write about these matters for a general audience is ferociously set upon by academics sniping away from within the ivy'd walls. When I published a story in the *New York Times Magazine* about developments at Duke, I was taken to task in *Dissent* by David Bromwich, a professor of English at Yale, who sneeringly referred to my work in the *New York Times* as "the Intellectual Beat" and made fun of the *Times Magazine* for having "taken a noticeable interest in culture, lately" (would it be better if we took no interest in culture?); rebuked in the *Chronicle of Higher Education* by a professor from a California polytechnical college who interviewed my sources in a failed effort to find instances of misquotation; and deconstructed in *Critical Inquiry* by a professor at Johns Hopkins who purported to show his readers what my article was *really* about, offering pseudo-sociological interpretations of the "text" and dismissing my article as an example of "corporate populism"—"the endeavor to make an appeal to the broadest possible sector of readers in a manner ostensibly without ideological prejudice. . . ." What's wrong with that?

Still, the level of debate has often been exhilaratingly high. To read the philosopher John Searle in the *New York Review of Books* on "The Storm over the University," or Irving Howe in the *New Republic* on "The Value of the Canon," or Louis Menand in *Harper's* on "What Is the University For?" is to find oneself in the presence of articulate moral passion. "Only in medicine are crises a sign of impending death," writes Paul Berman in the introduction to his lively anthology, *Debating P.C.* "In intellectual matters, crises are signs of life."

As I've followed this particular crisis over the last few years, nearly inundated by the flood of commentary, I've been heartened that so many feel so passionately about the issue—that there *is* a debate. It means that people are still interested in books. As the violence in our public high schools continues to escalate and our standards of literacy continue to decline, it can seem as if we're on the verge of a new barbarism, producing a generation of students who can't read and can't write, a generation connected to nothing; but I'm also impressed by the intensity of public commitment to the *idea* of education. If there's one thing everyone concerned with this issue is clear about, it's that we gain from the study of literature. Books alter the way we see ourselves. They form our collective character. We are what we read.

More than once, in the course of monitoring the curriculum debate, I've had an experience that seems to me fundamental to the process of education: the almost physical sensation of having one's mind changed. Irving Howe's moderate plea that there is such a thing as a common cultural heritage of mankind, and that children of all classes and ethnic types have profited immeasurably from knowing it, recognizes one truth; Stanley Fish's shrewd dismantlement of the assumptions behind our identification with that heritage in his essay "The Common Touch, or, One Size Fits All," recognizes another. The most eloquent commentators on this issue have also been the most persuasive.

Which doesn't mean that everyone is right. "All animals are equal, but some animals are more equal than others," according to the pigs' commandment in George Orwell's *Animal Farm*—a canonical text if there ever was one. No truth is self-evident; but some truths are more true than others. To question the inviolability of the literary canon, to examine its historical and ideological origins, to challenge its authority, can be an invigorating exercise; but it's possible to go too far. To banish the notion that education presupposes commitment to a shared tradition and shared ideals is to subvert its defining principle.

No one's asking for a consensus. Not even such a stern traditionalist as Cardinal John Henry Newman demanded it, as he made clear in *The Idea of a University:*

> The palaestra may seem a liberal exercise to Lycurgus, and illiberal to Seneca; coach-driving and prize-fighting may be recognized in Elis, and be condemned in England; music may be despicable in the eyes of certain moderns, and be in the highest place with Aristotle and Plato . . . still these variations imply, instead of discrediting, the archetypal idea, which is but a previous hypothesis or condition, by means of which issue is joined between contending opinions, and without which there would be nothing to dispute about.

By *archetype*, Newman meant the belief in a continuous historical tradition, however variously composed. Now even that belief is under attack. The insistence

upon a shared cultural tradition is ideologically suspect. Every effort to inculcate a body of knowledge
that reflects our common history is seen as an effort to
oppress. *A little learning is a dangerous thing:* this
aphorism is put forward without irony. If the curriculum debate can't settle the matter of what books our
children ought to read, or even why they ought to read
them, it can at least teach us how dangerous it is to
take anything for granted.

Battle of the Books

One

The Warning

In the fall of 1987 I joined the staff of the *New York Times Magazine.* Within a week of my arrival, a senior editor showed up from the third-floor newsroom to suggest that we do a story on Allan Bloom, a philosophy professor at the University of Chicago whose book *The Closing of the American Mind* had been at the top of the bestseller list for months. By the end of that year, it had sold close to a half-million copies. Bloom was America's latest intellectual celebrity: He was interviewed in *Time* magazine and seen on television talk shows. He was also a millionaire, no doubt a rarity among the high-minded members of the Committee on Social Thought.

No one can predict the public's taste. But *The Closing of the American Mind* has turned out to be more than one of those curious American phenomena, a book that captures a moment and acquires fleeting intellectual cachet, like Christopher Lasch's *The Culture of Narcissism* or Charles Reich's *The Greening of America*. Written, its author claimed, to please a few friends, Bloom's book was, and still is, a major event in American life. Five years after its publication, both the book and its author remain objects of intense debate. Bloom was the primary subject at a symposium entitled "The Humanities and the Question of Values in Education" held at Yale in the spring of 1989. A year later, at a symposium in Boston sponsored by *Partisan Review,* "The Changing Culture of the University," he still managed to draw the most fire. His intellectual presence hovers over Paul Berman's anthology, *Debating P.C.;* his entry in the index to *The Politics of Liberal Education,* edited by Darryl J. Gless and Barbara Herrnstein Smith, is large. By now, he's a venerable icon in the curriculum debate, a focus of inordinate attention and often venomous animosity. "To me," marvelled the philosopher John Searle in the *New York Review of Books,* "the amazing thing about Allan Bloom's book was not just its prodigious commercial success, but the depth of the hostility and even hatred that it inspired among a large number of professors." Whether or not *The Closing of the American Mind* will eventually turn out to be "another of those half-read bestsellers that plucks a momentary nerve, materializes fashionably on coffee tables, is rarely read all the way through, and is soon forgotten," as Arthur Schlesinger, Jr., has maintained, Bloom's eloquent polemic is clearly a phenomenon.

It wasn't a book that got raves, to say the least. Classicists faulted Bloom's scholarship, philosophers objected to his interpretations of philosophy, and educators disputed his contention that the universities were in a dreadful state. Commentators on the intellectual left were the most vociferous of all: they charged that Bloom was elitist, reactionary, and undemocratic. *The Closing of the American Mind* was a book that "decent people would be ashamed of having written," declared David Rieff in the *Times Literary Supplement* of London.

What was in this book that provoked such a storm? For one thing, Bloom wasn't so mild-mannered himself. In his survey of the American scene, he found much that was contemptible. Contemporary students are ignorant, he claimed; they don't read books; they're corrupted in adolescence by primitive rock music. One of Bloom's most notorious images was of a hypothetical thirteen-year-old boy doing his homework while listening to the "orgasmic rhythms" of a "drag queen" on his Walkman. "In short," he wrote, "life is made into a nonstop, commercially prepackaged masturbation fantasy." But it's not just the young who besmirch America; the culture as a whole is mediocre, "a Disneyland version of the Weimar Republic for the whole family."

The culprit, in Bloom's view, is cultural relativism: the notion that all societies, all cultures, all values are equal. They're not, Bloom insisted. Equality is "a democratic prejudice," an obstacle to the contemplation of higher things. "The real community of man," he concluded, "is the community of those who seek the truth, of the potential knowers, that is, in principle, of all men to the extent they desire to know." In truth, however, "this includes only a few."

How did the university figure in Bloom's scheme of things? His book was subtitled *How Higher Education Has Failed Democracy and Impoverished the Souls of Today's Students.* (Bloom must have gained confidence in his argument as the book made its way through the stages of publication: the subtitle in the galley was *Education and the Crisis of Reason.*) Bloom deplored the low standards that prevail these days on American campuses. Who's to blame? College administrators, who have abdicated their civilizing role by acquiescing to the demand for "relevance." The "radicalization" of the curriculum was, in Bloom's opinion, a plot to discredit the classics—what they call around the University of Chicago the Great Books.

Bloom himself had grown up on those books, and it showed. He didn't wear his scholarship lightly. *The Closing of the American Mind* is an engaging book, crammed with anecdotes and lively personal digressions, but it's not an easy read. The table of contents— "The Nietzscheanization of the Left or Vice Versa," "From Socrates' *Apology* to Heidegger's *Rektoratsrede*"—reflects the density of Bloom's argument. Nor was his thesis entirely new. That the universities were in trouble had been known in the universities for quite a while. Five years earlier, the eminent biographer and Harvard professor of English Walter Jackson Bate had warned in a famous essay, "The Crisis in English Studies," that the humanities were "plunging into their worst state of crisis since the modern university was formed a century ago." Students of literature no longer had even a rudimentary grasp of the works they used to read as a matter of course, Bate lamented. They knew virtually nothing of history, of foreign languages and literatures, even of their own language and literature.

It was the way Bloom said it that touched a nerve. Instead of supplying statistics about the dwindling capabilities of students, he conjured up a vision of encroaching barbarism. Debunking the 1960s, with its heavy emphasis on equality, democracy, and the rights of the many as opposed to the few, he disparaged with lip-curling verve the cultural vacuity of a generation numbed by rock music: "Mick Jagger played the role in their lives that Napoleon played in the lives of ordinary young Frenchmen throughout the nineteenth century." What had the 1960s actually produced in the way of culture? Not a whole lot, according to Bloom. "Not a single book of lasting importance was produced in or around the movement." Works of supposedly radical philosophy by those fashionable intellectual gurus Herbert Marcuse and Norman O. Brown were in fact spurious adaptations of German philosophy. If there was a decade to celebrate, Bloom argued, it was the 1950s, "one of the great periods of the American university," when many of the European scholars who had fled Hitler in great numbers did their most important work: "They initiated us into a tradition that was living and that penetrated the tastes and standards of society at large."

If you happened to believe in Bloom's thesis, this was provocative stuff. If you didn't, it was offensive. Either way, his argument engaged significant issues— what Bloom himself likes to call the Big Questions. "Every educational system has a moral goal that it tries to attain and that informs its curriculum," he wrote. Clearly, that system wasn't working. Moral goals had been sacrificed to new political expediencies; the universities were ruled by special-interest groups, each lobbying for its own discipline—black studies, women's studies, Asian-American studies. "America has no-fault automobile accidents, no-fault divorces, and it is moving with the aid of modern philosophy toward no-fault choices." The new all-inclusive curriculum was like the Nature Theater of Oklahoma in Franz Kafka's novel *Amerika*, where "everyone is welcome, everyone can be an artist." In the universities of the 1980s, every culture was welcome.

For Bloom, the implication of all this was clear: the barbarians were at the gate, ready to storm the walled fortress where he did his work. One of the most moving passages in *The Closing of the American Mind* was Bloom's evocation of what the university had meant to him in his youth: "When I was 15 years old I saw the University of Chicago for the first time and somehow sensed that I had discovered my life. I had never before seen, or at least had not noticed, buildings that were evidently dedicated to a higher purpose, not to necessity or utility, not merely to shelter or manufacture or trade, but to something that might be an end in itself." The millionaires—John D. Rockefeller, the McCormicks and other wealthy Chicago families—who had financed a world-class university in their midst "paid tribute to what they had neglected," Bloom surmised, "whether it was out of a sense of what they themselves had missed, or out of bad conscience about what their lives were exclusively devoted to, or to satisfy the vanity of having their names attached to the enterprise." In the end, it hardly mattered why. The university was there. "Education was an American thing."

Assigned to write a profile of Bloom, I spent an exhilarating week in Hyde Park. I sat in on his class, taking notes like everyone else, while he strode back and forth before the podium, smoking and discoursing in his voluble stammer on Rousseau's *Emile*. It was tonic to be out of the pressured realm of New York, where no one has time to read anything but magazines. Browsing in the secondhand bookstores around the university, I was reminded of how much books had once meant to me—not the new releases that I read about in *Publishers' Weekly*, but the old books, the books I'd read in college, for general edification, to satisfy (Bloom has revived the word) my soul.

Yet Bloom inhabited no ivory tower. Following his own passions, scribbling late at night in his Chicago high-rise, he had stumbled upon a hot topic. His book was more than a professor's sour diatribe against rock 'n' roll. It was a warning. What was happening on American campuses, according to Bloom, reflected developments in the culture at large. The Great Books were more than books; they were the essence of all that mattered in Western civilization, the highest expression of our "human desire to know." To produce a generation of students ignorant of those books would have grim consequences in the world beyond the college walls. There was a connection between philosophy and politics, between the life of the mind—in Bloom's opinion, the only meaningful life—and the life of the commonwealth. The decline of educational standards portended the decline of the West. Just as the universities had failed to affirm the supremacy of the values it was their mandate to protect, so had the United States abdicated its role in foreign affairs. "This is the American moment in world history," Bloom cautioned, "the one for which we shall forever be judged." Nations are no more relative than cultures; some are destined to lead, others to follow. In short—to use one of Bloom's favorite locutions— we're number one. Or were.

My article appeared in a January 1988 issue of the *New York Times Magazine,* with a photograph of Bloom on the cover, cigarette in hand, in one of his elegant French-cut suits. The headline was CHICAGO'S GRUMPY GURU. But it wasn't until later that year, when I began preliminary work for an article about the curriculum debates that were happening around the country, that I began to sense what was at issue. Walking back to his apartment one afternoon, Bloom had shown me a clipping from that day's *New York Times* that described a flap at Stanford, where a plan was under way to revise the series of Western civilization courses required of freshmen, paring down the core list of classics and substituting works by "women, minorities, and persons of color." "Look at this!" Bloom exclaimed, halting beneath a streetlamp to marvel again at the scrap of paper in his hand. "And people think I exaggerate!"

By that spring, the curriculum was news. Washington's policymakers seized upon the events at Stanford as an opportunity to scold the universities. Lynne V. Cheney, chairman of the National Endowment for the Humanities, drafted a pamphlet, *Humanities in America,* that contained some very bad tidings indeed. Subtitled "A Report to the President, the Congress, and the American People," Cheney's trenchant essay made the case that academic departments in history, literature, and the arts were becoming at once overly specialized and lax in their standards. Campus observers had noted an atmosphere of "disarray and isolation," she reported. "They have written of a lost sense of meaning in academic studies." She cited ominous statistics: Between 1966 and 1986 the number of bachelor's degrees awarded by American universities increased by 88 percent; in the humanities, they decreased by 33 percent. It was possible to receive a diploma from the vast majority of four-year colleges and universities without having taken a single course in Western civilization, American history, or a foreign language. "Do students learn how the ideals and practices of our civilization have evolved?" asked Cheney. "Do they take away from their undergraduate years a sense of the interconnection of ideas and events—a framework into which they can fit the learning of a lifetime?" Not the way matters stood now. The notion that there existed a hierarchy of knowledge, a cultural tradition made up of the best that is known and thought in the world, was a thing of the past.

William Bennett, then secretary of education, was equally dire. "The West is the culture in which we live," he told an audience at Stanford in the spring of 1988. "It has set the moral, political, economic, and social standards for the rest of the world." In bowing to the vocal band of student radicals that had demanded a new, more relevant curriculum, Bennett asserted, "a great university was brought low by the very forces which modern universities came into being to oppose: ignorance, irrationality, and intimidation."

Bennett's outburst, like Bloom's book, created a loud outcry. All over the country, editorials appeared denouncing the sorry developments at Stanford, where students on a 1987 march with Jesse Jackson had chanted, "Hey hey, ho, ho, Western culture's gotta go." Universities in America have always been viewed with a certain amount of suspicion, idealized as places of higher learning but not entirely respected; they're too far from the sources of wealth and power. But at least they were tolerated as a supposedly civilizing influence. Now it seemed as if they had a very different mission. The defenders of high culture were in the real world, in journalism and government; the philistines were in the university. Bloom and Bennett became a synecdoche for the old guard: standard-bearers opposed to curriculum reform and the menace to Western culture it represented. (In the academic world, they were known as the Killer B's.)

On campus, meanwhile, administrators were scrambling to invent courses that would fill the new demand for cultural diversity. At Stanford, a requirement known as Culture/Ideas/Values (CIV) supplanted the old Western culture curriculum, stipulating the inclusion of courses that would "confront issues relating to class, ethnicity, race, religion, gender, and sexual orientation." At Berkeley, the cradle of student radicalism during the 1960s, home of the original Free-Speech Movement, the faculty voted to adopt a new requirement. Freshmen or sophomores would have to pass a one-semester course focusing on at least three out of five ethnic groups: African-Americans, Latinos, Asian-Americans, Native Americans, and European-Americans.

But the curricular debate was more than a matter of placating various ethnic groups. In 1988 the Yale professor and critic Paul de Man made posthumous headlines when it was discovered that he had written a number of anti-Semitic articles for Nazi-controlled periodicals in Belgium during World War II. In his new incarnation as an Ivy League academic, de Man had been one of the most influential proponents of deconstructionism, a literary theory that insists upon the "indeterminacy of the text." Language is incapable of saying what it means to say, claim the deconstructionists; the author invariably reveals motives, or intentions, that elude his conscious design; the act of critical interpretation is fatally flawed by the reader's own presuppositions, or "blindness." Language and literature can never be put in the service of truth because it is impossible to determine what the truth is: a work of art is beyond interpretation.

A year later, Francis Fukuyama, then a State Department official, generated a vast amount of coverage in the press with an article portentously called "The End of History?" (It has since been expanded into a best-selling book entitled *The End of History and the Last Man;* the question mark is gone, suggesting either that the author is more confident of his thesis now or that history really *has* come to an end.) Published in the *National Interest,* Fukuyama's essay was a shrewd effort to translate Bloom's ideas into the realm of politics. To all appearances, Fukuyama was optimistic; in the twentieth century, he argued, the forces of totalitarianism have been decisively conquered by the United States and its allies, which represent the final embodiment of history—"that is, the end point of mankind's ideological evolution and the universalization of Western liberal democracy." In other words, we win.

Not so fast. The end of history, according to Fukuyama, would be "a very sad time." The "emptiness at the core of liberalism" would become drearily apparent. The triumph of democracy would usher in a "consumerist culture" purveying rock music around the world. Where had I heard this rhetoric before? It turned out that Fukuyama had been a student of Bloom's at Cornell. He had also been a graduate student in comparative literature at Yale, where he studied with Paul de Man.

From deconstructionism to the highest levels of

government, from literary theory to foreign policy—I was beginning to get the drift. The attack on the meaning of a literary text—on its authority—was analogous to the attack on political authority that had begun in the 1960s, and that Fukuyama now deplored. Deconstructionism had its origin in Continental philosophy; so did the campus riots of the 1960s, at least in Bloom's version of things. America may have triumphed in the economic and military spheres, but it had failed in the educational sphere. Indeed, the universities were busy working to undermine the very values for which they had once stood. And it wasn't just the universities. The same thing was happening everywhere. America was on the way down. It was hollow at the core.

"What do Shakespeare and Milton have to do with solving our problems?" Bloom asked in *The Closing of the American Mind*. As it happens, everything.

Two

The Big Boys

The philosopher George Santayana was once asked which books young people ought to read. It didn't matter, he replied, as long as they read the same ones. Generations of college students followed his advice. In the standard introductory course to Western civ you read some Greek philosophy, the Bible, St. Augustine, Machiavelli, Rousseau, Marx, and John Stuart Mill. If it was a literature course, you read Chaucer, Shakespeare, Milton, the Romantic poets, the Victorian novelists . . . and so on, century by century, masterpiece by masterpiece, until you'd read (or browsed through) the corpus. The best that has been thought and said.

The best, like everything else, was susceptible to fashion. Occasional disputes broke out, reputations waxed and waned. T. S. Eliot restored the luster of the seventeenth-century metaphysical poets; the literary critic Malcolm Cowley promoted Faulkner; there was a Henry James revival. For the most part, though, you were either on the syllabus or off the syllabus.

What *is* the best that has been thought and said? Gerald Graff, a professor of English at the University of Chicago and one of the most articulate commentators on the curriculum debate, observes that the trouble with this "Matthew Arnold view of literature and culture" is that there never was any consensus about what it means to be educated in our society. The idea of literature as a fixed and immutable canon—the Great Books, the Five-Foot Shelf—is a historical illusion. "Canon-busting is nothing new," says Graff. "There have always been politics. Teaching Shakespeare instead of the classics was a radical innovation."

Teaching literature was once an innovation. Until the late nineteenth century, philology—the linguistic analysis of literature—was the closest thing to literary studies in the university. Rhetoric, oratory, Greek, and Latin dominated the syllabus. It wasn't until about the 1880s that literature as we now know it became a proper subject of study, and even then scholars were mostly textual exegetes, devoted to the preparation of new editions of the classics. The idea that literature could serve as a guide to the conduct of life, an interpretation of culture, had no place in the university. This was a field reserved for critics: generalists like Henry Wadsworth Longfellow and James Russell Lowell, who wrote for wide-circulation magazines and decried the professionalism of their academic colleagues.

Literature as linguistics—the "philological syndicate," as Harry Levin, the distinguished professor emeritus of comparative literature at Harvard, has described it—was eventually superseded by the New Criticism of poet-critics like John Crowe Ransom and Allen Tate, who both taught in universities and addressed themselves to a wider literary audience. They, too, were devoted to close reading, or analysis, of texts; but they ventured beyond the classics. Their most famous essays are about the English poets, and those were the poets they taught. By the 1940s, literature as it was studied by undergraduates meant English and American literature, supplemented by works in translation.

When I was a freshman at Harvard in 1967, the English literature courses listed in the catalogue were more or less the same ones that had been offered for decades (and so were the professors): "Biblical Symbolism in English Literature," "English Poetry and Prose of the Romantic Period," "English Poetry: Dryden to Wordsworth," "The Nineteenth-Century English Novel." There were some hip courses, like "The Modern Sensibility," in which we read Yeats and Freud; *Love's Body* by Norman O. Brown; *Tristes Tropiques*, the autobiography of Claude Lévi-Strauss;

and Ludwig Wittgenstein's *Tractatus.* But you also needed a certain number of credits in English literature to get a degree; you needed to know at least one foreign language; and you had to demonstrate some acquaintance with *The Norton Anthology of English Literature.*

Even then, there was spirited debate about the purpose of education—not only what books a student ought to read, but what kinds of values those books were meant to inculcate. The question, as Lionel Trilling framed it in a prophetic lecture, "The Uncertain Future of the Humanistic Educational Ideal," was a practical one: "What is best for young minds to be engaged by, how they may best be shaped through what they read—or look at or listen to—and think about." At Columbia, where Trilling studied and where he taught for a half-century, the Great Books Program, as it came to be known there, was firmly enshrined. The study of the "whole man"—that is to say, history, ethics, and philosophy, as well as literature—was standard procedure. ("No one then thought of the necessity of saying the 'whole person,'" Trilling noted dryly.)

By the 1960s, the whole-man idea had been scaled down considerably. It was possible to earn a bachelor of arts degree without a lot of sweat. I recall my panic when called upon in a final exam to discuss works from the three principal phases of Shakespeare's career. Having consulted previous exams— they were available in the library for that purpose—I had taken my cue from the Shakespeare question of the year before and boned up on one play from each of the four principal genres: comedy, tragedy, history, and romance. I wrote about genre—and got a decent grade. The experience was a vivid confirmation that not much was expected of us. If you happened to read a few of the books they asked you to read, fine. If not, also fine.

What my classmates and I managed to learn in those four years couldn't begin to compare with the knowledge absorbed by earlier generations of students, for whom the study of literature included the study of Greek and Latin classics in the original. But at least the idea of general education was intact. No one disputed that there were Great Books. No one doubted that it was a good thing to have some grasp of what Western culture was all about—whether or not we had any grasp of it ourselves.

The curriculum wasn't an issue then. Our demands (as we defined student protest at Harvard) were explicitly political. They focused on the draft, ROTC, the Vietnam War, the ethics of military research and the universities' investment policies, the grievances of the (usually poor and black) communities on their perimeters. Not that the members of Students for a Democratic Society (SDS), the main organization of campus radicals, were doctrinaire Marxists; their meetings and demonstrations were often suffused with a distinctly countercultural aura. STRIKE BECAUSE THERE'S NO POETRY IN YOUR LIFE, read the motto on posters and T-shirts adorned with a clenched red fist in the spring of 1969. But politics was an extracurricular activity; in the library, we still read Locke and Hobbes.

The faculty grasped the implications of the student movement more quickly than its instigators did. "The past five years have been, for American universities, the most dramatic in our history," wrote Daniel Bell and Irving Kristol in their preface to *Confrontation: The Student Rebellion and the University* (1969). Dramatic and devastating, from their point of view: what was happening in that turbulent era was nothing less than the destruction of the university and of the civilization whose noblest monuments of learning it was the university's mandate to preserve. "Not since the civil conflict of a century ago has this country, as I see it, been in such great danger," warned the American diplomat George Kennan in a 1968 essay prompted by the events at Columbia. The ideals of "commitment, duty, self-restraint" that higher education was supposed to encourage in the young had been sacrificed, said Kennan, in the name of a spurious personal freedom masquerading as politics.

The danger passed. By the mid-1970s, the campus violence of a few years before was history. The gun-toting black students who occupied an administration building at Cornell in 1969 had put away their weapons; SDS had become a fringe group on the left. Within a few years, half a decade if that, the momentous events my generation witnessed—the assassinations of King and Kennedy, the March on Washington, the Chicago convention of 1968—had become oddly remote. The Republicans were back in office, and people were transfixed by the Watergate hearings. It was as if the 1960s had never happened.

Yet the student movement left its mark. Afro-

American departments were a feature of most universities; ROTC was gone, or on the way out; the Vietnam War was over. On campus, the most enduring legacy of that decade was to be found in the curriculum. "During the '60s I sat on various committees at Cornell and continuously and futilely voted against dropping one requirement after the next," Bloom recalled. "The old core curriculum—according to which every student in the college had to take a smattering of courses in the major divisions of knowledge—was abandoned." What was left was "a threadbare reminiscence of the unity of knowledge" that had been the university's original purpose and ideal.

At least it was a reminiscence. In the aftermath of the 1960s, students of literature were indoctrinated with a method that was, if anything, *more* esoteric than the New Criticism it supplanted: deconstructionism. This would become the dominant mode of literary criticism and practice within the academy. By the 1970s, no one was just reading anymore; everyone was deconstructing.

There was nothing simple about the new discipline. Indeed, its vocabulary was so difficult, so willfully abstract, that only initiates could decipher its primary "texts" (or books, as they used to be called). "As seen from the public perspective of literary journalists and literary critics, the disputes among literary theorists more and more appear to be like quarrels among theologians, at the furthest remove from any reality or practicality," began one of Paul de Man's late essays, entitled "Hypogram and Inscription." The same essay ended with a sentence that seemed as if it had been

written to confirm the suspicions of the very constituency that de Man belittled (if any representative of it
got that far): "Inscription is neither a figure, nor a
sign, nor a cognition, nor a desire, nor a hypogram, nor
a matrix, yet no theory of reading or of poetry can
achieve consistency if it responds to its powers only by
a figural invasion which, in this case, takes the subtly
effective form of evading the figural." In other words
(I think), works of literature don't necessarily say
what their authors intended them to say.

What was radical about this innovative method
was its premise: namely, that the impulse to interpret
works of literature is itself political. Literary criticism
is "strategic, a violent and bloody act," according to
de Man. To deconstruct a text is to question its literal
meaning, the validity of its authorial point of view—to
challenge its intention. "All language is about language," de Man insisted. Interpreting Shelley's poem
"The Triumph of Life," he found that its imagery was
largely unconscious, its logic impaired. The poem
didn't track. Shelley's description of dawn made it
seem as if that natural phenomenon, "the most continuous and gradual event in nature," happened all at
once: ". . . the sun sprang forth." The image, noted de
Man, is "brusque and unmotivated." How could it be
otherwise? "Language posits and language means
(since it articulates), but language cannot posit meaning; it can only reiterate (or reflect) it in its recon-
firmed falsehood." In other words, Shelley didn't
know what he was doing.

Yet even deconstructionism, subversive as it was,
concentrated its deconstructive—that is to say, its de-
structive—energies on traditional works. The texts de

Man taught—Wordsworth, Blake, Yeats—were the
same ones an earlier generation of critics had inter-
preted in its own fashion. It wasn't the curriculum
that had changed; it was our way of reading the books
that composed it.

It wasn't until the mid-1980s that real trouble
broke out. My first intimation of it was in the academic journals: I kept stumbling across references to
the *canon*. Originally a Greek term—*kanon*—em-
ployed by Alexandrian scholars in second- and third-
century Greece, it meant "a straight rod," "a ruler,"
"a standard," and was a compilation of works, in
prose and poetry, that were considered the best examples of each genre. Later on, the word came to refer to
those works that the church considered part of the
Bible. Now, apparently, it had a new meaning.
PMLA, the journal of the Modern Language Association, proposed an issue on "the idea of the literary
canon in relation to concepts of judgment, taste, and
value." In the spring of 1988, the Princeton English
department held a symposium entitled "Masterpieces: Canonizing the Literary."

Canon formation, canon revision, canonicity: the
mysterious, often indecipherable language of criticism
had yielded up a whole new terminology. What was
this canon? The books that constituted the intellectual
heritage of educated Americans, that had officially
been defined as great. The kind of books you read,
say, in Columbia's famed lit hum course, virtually un-
changed since 1937: Homer, Plato, Dante, Milton.
The masterpieces of Western Civilization. The Big
Boys.

In the academic world, I kept hearing, the canon

was *the* issue. "Everything these days has to do with the canon," one of my campus sources reported. Then came Bloom and Bennett. By the spring of 1988, "canon politics" was in the news. "From Western lit to Westerns as lit," joked the *Wall Street Journal* in a piece about some English professors down at Duke who were teaching *The Godfather* (both the book and the movie), *E.T.*, and the novels of Louis L'Amour. An article in the *New York Times* entitled "U.S. Literature: Canon Under Siege" quoted a heretical brigade of academics who were fed up with literary-value hierarchies. Why should Melville and Emerson dominate the syllabus? argued renegade professors from Princeton and Duke. What about Zora Neale Hurston, a heroine of the Harlem renaissance? What about Harriet Beecher Stowe? "It's no different from choosing between a hoagie and a pizza," explained Houston Baker, a professor of literature at the University of Pennsylvania.

Up at Harvard, nothing had changed in Warren House, the colonial clapboard dwelling across from the Student Union, where I'd gone for tutorials with Robert Fitzgerald, the late Boylston Professor of English and translator of the *Odyssey*, twenty years ago. The stuffy, low-ceilinged rooms with their worn Persian carpets and book-crammed mahogany shelves were just as I remembered them. Only the catalogue I'd gone there to obtain one afternoon was different. "Courses of Instruction 1988–1989" was as bewildering a volume as any text by Paul de Man. On the cover was that reassuring logo : VERITAS. I turned to the listings under English and American Literature and

Language. There was "Old English Literature in Translation," still taught by the playwright and Harvard legend William Alfred. There was "The Age of Johnson" and "English Romantic Poetry." But what was this? "Virginia Woolf and Toni Morrison"? A course on Southern fiction that included Ellen Gilchrist and Alice Walker? "Modern American Poetry," taught by no less an authority than Helen Vendler, that included Dave Smith, Jorie Graham, and Rita Dove?

It wasn't only the new—in some cases unknown—names that stopped me. The course descriptions were just as strange. My eye fell upon "Literature and Human Suffering," a course on "Tolstoy, Hardy, Melville, Douglass, Solzhenitsyn, and writers dealing with slavery and the Holocaust." Then there was "Representations of Family and Kinship in the Eighteenth-Century Novel," described as "an investigation of the treatment of family relations and sexuality," of "incest as a narrative trope." "The Politics of Childbirth and Childhood in Anglo-American Literature" proposed for study *Alice in Wonderland, The Land of Oz,* and *The Bluest Eye.* Even the traditional courses promised untraditional approaches: "Problems in Shakespearean Interpretation," for instance, would address "questions opened by feminism, new historicism, materialism, deconstruction, psychoanalysis, and other post-structuralist ways of reading and interpreting."

Amazing! In just two decades, the teaching of literature—the values it was supposed to inculcate, the questions it was supposed to answer, the very books themselves—had been transformed. What mattered now was *contextualization:* establishing a work in its historical context. Literature as sociology—that was the new game. Consider, for instance, English 90cd, "Literature, Politics, and the English Revolution": ". . . an examination of the rich variety of texts—literary, sub-literary, political—which refract in diverse ways the experience and culture of Interregnum England." I read on: "Women and Culture in Victorian Society," "Black and White in American Culture," "Innocence and Violence in America," "The Rise of Mass Culture." It all sounded very interesting. The only thing missing was the books.

Well, what of it? There was a long tradition of studying literature in this way. Marx and his disciples had contributed a great deal in the line of literary criticism, from *Leon Trotsky on Literature and Art* to the writings of Walter Benjamin, from Hannah Arendt to Edward Said. Edmund Wilson, by consensus America's greatest literary critic, was a diligent historian; his most important books, *To the Finland Station* and *Patriotic Gore*, are models of how to write about literature against the backdrop of history.

Only it wasn't just history that dominated literature now; it was politics. The whole idea behind the new curriculum, I gathered from my own close reading of the Harvard catalogue, was to recognize and identify the ideological forces that produced a work of art. It was the context they were looking at: what a book—any book—said about society. "Modern experimental novels considered as explorations of shifting racial and sexual relations." "An investigation of the treatment of family relations and sexuality in a number of eighteenth-century novels." "Selected autobiographies raise issues of nationalism, race, gender, and American self-styling. . . ."

I remembered a line of Yeats (was he still taught?): "The world is changed, changed utterly."

Three

The New
Canonists

O n the shelves in Jane Tompkins's office at Duke
are rows of nineteenth-century novels; she is
one of the few who reads them now. Her book *Sensational Designs: The Cultural Work of American Fiction 1790–1860* is a brilliant exhumation of what she
considers lost masterpieces, the history of a different
American literature from the one I read in college
twenty years ago.

Writers like Charles Brockden Brown, Harriet
Beecher Stowe, and Susan Warner still deserve an au-

dience, Tompkins argues with considerable persuasiveness. If they're no longer read, it's because our values have changed. The way to read these books is from the vantage of the past. Only by reconstructing the culture in which they were written and the audience to whom they were addressed can we learn to appreciate their intrinsic worth and see them for what they are: "man-made, historically produced objects" whose reputations were created in their day by a powerful literary establishment. In other words, the Great Books aren't the only books.

Tompkins is one of the jewels in the crown of Duke's English department, which in the last few years has assembled a faculty that can now claim to rival any in the country. Attracted by salaries that in some cases approach six figures and a university willing to let them teach pretty much whatever interests them, the new recruits compose a formidable team: Frank Lentricchia, the author of *After the New Criticism* and other works; Fredric Jameson, probably the foremost Marxist critic in the country; Barbara Herrnstein Smith, a former president of the Modern Language Association; and Jane Tompkins's husband, Stanley Fish, a professor of both English and Law, and a very public figure in the curriculum debate. (Duke is known in academic circles as the Fish Tank.)

Canon revision is in full swing down at Duke, where students lounge about the manicured quad of the imitation-Cotswold campus and the magnolias blossom in the spring. In the Duke catalogue, the English department lists, besides the usual offerings in Chaucer and Shakespeare, courses entitled "American Popular Culture," "Advertising and Society," "Television, Technology, and Culture." Lentricchia teaches a course entitled "Paranoia, Politics, and Other Pleasures" that focuses on the works of Joan Didion, Don DeLillo, and Michel Foucault. Tompkins, an avid reader of contemporary fiction—on a shelf in her office I spotted copies of *Princess Daisy* and *Valley of the Dolls*—is teaching all kinds of things, from a course on American literature and culture in the 1850s to one called "Home on the Range: The Western in American Culture."

Tompkins talks about her work with a rhetorical intensity that reminds me of the fervent Students for a Democratic Society types I used to know in college. Like so many of those in the vanguard of the new canonical insurrection, she is a child of the sixties and a dedicated feminist. In *Sensational Designs*, she recounts how she gradually became aware of herself as a woman working in a "male-dominated scholarly tradition that controls both the canon of American literature and the critical perspective that interprets the canon for society." The writers offered up as classics didn't speak to Tompkins; they didn't address her own experience. "If you look at the names on Butler Library up at Columbia, they're all white males," she notes one afternoon over lunch in the faculty dining hall. "We wanted to talk about civil rights in the classroom, to prove that literature wasn't a sacred icon above the heat and dust of conflict."

The English-literature syllabus, Tompkins and her colleagues on other campuses discovered, was a potential instrument of change: "This is where it all came out in the wash." By the 1970s, women's studies majors had been installed on college campuses across the land. Books on gender, race, and ethnicity poured from the university presses. Seminars were offered in Native American literature, Hispanic literature, and Asian-American literature. "It wasn't only women we'd neglected," says Marjorie Garber, director of the Harvard Center for Literary and Cultural Studies. "It was the whole Third World."

The ideology behind these challenges to the canon is as obvious as the vanity plates on Frank Lentricchia's old Dodge: GO LEFT. Pick up any recent academic journal and you'll find it packed with articles on "Maidens, Maps, and Mines: The Reinvention of Patriarchy in Colonial South Africa" or "Dominance, Hegemony, and the Modes of Minority Discourse." The critical vocabulary of the 1980s bristles with militant neologisms: *Eurocentrism, phallocentrism, logophallocentrism* (why not *Europhallologocentrism*?). "This is not an intellectual agenda; it is a political agenda," former secretary of education William Bennett declared.

Why should a revolutionary curricular struggle be happening at a time when radical politics in America is virtually extinct? Walk into any classroom and you'll find the answer. Enormous sociological changes have occurred in American universities over the last twenty years; the ethnic profile of both students and faculty has undergone a dramatic transformation. There's a higher proportion of minorities in college than ever before. By the end of this century, Hispanic, black, and Asian-American undergraduates at Stanford will outnumber whites. Their professors, many of whom were on the barricades in the 1960s, are now up for tenure. "It's a demographic phenomenon," Jane Tompkins says. "There are women, Jews, Italians teaching literature in universities. The people who are teaching now don't look the way professors used to look. Frank Lentricchia doesn't look like Cleanth Brooks."

I had never seen Cleanth Brooks, the eminent Yale professor emeritus, but I could imagine him striding across campus in a conservative gray suit and neat bow tie—not at all the way Frank Lentricchia looks. The photograph on the book jacket of *Criticism and Social Change* shows a guy in a sports shirt, posed against a graffiti-scarred wall—"the Dirty Harry of contemporary critical theory," a reviewer in the *Village Voice* called him.

In person, Lentricchia is a lot less intimidating. I found him mild-mannered, easygoing, and surprisingly conventional in his approach to literature. Standing before his modern poetry class in a faded blue work shirt open at the neck, he made his way through *The Waste Land* just the way professors used to, line by line, pointing out the buried allusions to Ovid and Dante, Marvell and Verlaine. His work is densely theoretical, yet there's nothing doctrinaire about it. What comes through is a devotion to the classics that is more visceral than abstract. "I'm interested in social issues as they bear on literature, but what really interests me is the mainline stuff, like Faulkner," he says after class, popping open a beer—no sherry—on the porch of his comfortable home in the nearby town of Hillsboro. "I'm too American to be a Marxist."

One afternoon I talked with Stanley Fish in his newly renovated office in the Allen Building. Fish had on slacks and a sports jacket, but he didn't look any more like Cleanth Brooks, or my image of Cleanth Brooks, than Frank Lentricchia does. He's never been at ease with the English tradition, he said, though he's one of the leading Milton scholars in America.

Now in his mid-fifties, Fish is maybe a decade older than the generation of radical scholars that came of age in the 1960s; but like many of them, he discovered his vocation largely on his own. "You come from a background where there were no books, the son of immigrants," he says. In such a world, Milton was a first name.

For American writers who grew up in the Depression, the art critic Clement Greenberg once noted, literature offered "a means of flight from the restriction and squalor of the Brooklyns and Bronxes to the wide-open world which rewards the successful fugitive with space, importance, and wealth." Making it in those days meant making it on others' terms: in Fish's case, the terms established by tradition-minded English departments dominated by white Anglo-Saxon Protestants, which only a few decades ago looked with skeptical distaste upon the Jewish assistant professors who were trying to storm the gates. Diana Trilling has written movingly about the humiliations her celebrated husband, Lionel, suffered at the beginning of his career, when he was briefly banished from Columbia by the English department on the grounds that he was "a Freudian, a Marxist, and a Jew." There was nothing subversive about Trilling's ambition; for him, as for Jewish critics like Philip Rahv and Alfred Kazin, literature was a means of escape from the constraints of ethnic identity, not an affirmation of it. They never denied their Jewishness; they simply considered themselves Americans and writers first.

Fish and his radical colleagues are no less ambitious. They, too, aspire to "space, importance, and wealth," but on their own terms. Frank Lentricchia writes openly and with unashamed ardor, in the autobiographical fashion of the day, about his Italian-American origins, his grandfather in Utica, and his working-class dad. "To become an intellectual from this kind of background means typically to try to forget where you've come from," he notes in *Criticism and Social Change*. It means becoming "a cosmopolitan gentleman of the world of letters, philosophy, and art." That's not Lentricchia's style. For the radical scholars of his generation, it's no longer a matter of proving their claim on literature; that struggle has been won. What they're demanding now is a literature that reflects their experience, a literature of their own. "Assimilation is a betrayal," says Fish. "The whole idea of 'Americanness' has been thrown in question."

A recent anthology published by the Graywolf Press in St. Paul, Minnesota, confirms this development. Entitled *Multi-Cultural Literacy: Opening the American Mind,* it makes deliberate reference to the two best-selling books that brought the revolution in the humanities to the attention of a larger public:

Bloom's *Closing of the American Mind* and E. D. Hirsch's *Cultural Literacy*. *Multi-Cultural Literacy* is a populist anthology, an alternative to the "institutionalized racism" of the curriculum, with its "white, male, academic, eastern U.S., Eurocentric bias." Where on Hirsch's list of "What Every American Needs to Know" is the *Bhagavad Gita?* Where is *One Hundred Years of Solitude?* Rhythm and blues? El Salvador? Rooted in the politics of the 1960s, *Multi-Cultural Literacy* might as well be called *Countercultural Literacy*. Among its contents is an essay by Paula Gunn Allen, "Who Is Your Mother? Red Roots of White Feminism," that offers an "Indian-focused version" of American history, designed to reaffirm the important place of women in the structure of tribal society; an essay by the black writer Ishmael Reed, "America: The Multinational Society," celebrating the "cultural bouillabaisse" of a nation where Yoruban, an African dialect, is spoken at a conference of African-American scholars in Milwaukee; and a list, modeled after Hirsch's, that includes Black Elk, Bo Diddley, Jack Kerouac, and Tonto. (That's right, Tonto.)

It's not only the literature syllabus that reflects this cultural counterinsurgency; the emphasis on minority cultures has pervaded the university. "What used to attract people to sociology is that we were able to look at blacks and Jews and Italians and see what is universal," says Egon Mayer, a professor of sociology at Brooklyn College. "Now those same students, who are Jews and blacks, want to study what's unique about themselves."

In history, which has gone the way of literature and sociology, there's even a term for this intellectual trend: "history from below." The old history—elitist history, or "history from above"—studied kings, presidents, political leaders, and thinkers. The New History studies the anonymous masses: slaves, peasants, criminals, and the insane. Popular culture, the plight of women, the struggles of oppressed classes: these have now become the subject of legitimate inquiry for historians. "Mickey Mouse may in fact be more important to understanding the 1930s than Franklin Roosevelt," as one New Historian has put it. "The history of menarche is equal in importance to the history of monarchy," declares another.

The old-fashioned approach to literature and history, says Ishmael Reed, is a myth invented by Ivy League professors in order to impose their "small-screen view of political and cultural reality upon a complex world." Let's put behind us "the antebellum aesthetic position," advises Henry Louis Gates, Jr., the W.E.B. Du Bois Professor of Literature at Harvard University. decrying the days when "scholar-critics were white men and when women and people of other color were voiceless, faceless servants and laborers, pouring tea and filling brandy snifters in the boardrooms of old boys' clubs." Culture is a form of enslavement. The canon is just another racist scam.

In a way, this was what the debate at Stanford was about. "If you think we are talking about a handful of good books, you are mistaken," Bill King, a senior and president of the university's black-student union, declared in the spring of 1988, imploring the faculty senate to vote for a new curriculum. "We are discussing the foundations of education in America and the acceptance of Euro-America's place in the world as contributor, not creator." Why had he never been taught that Socrates, Herodotus, Pythagoras, and Solon owed much of what they knew to African cultures in Egypt, or that many of the words of Solomon were borrowed from the Egyptian writer Amen-En-Eope? Where, in the great scheme of things, were *his* people to be found?

To someone brought up on the idea that assimilation was an essential component of the American experience—that what established one's identity was the convergence, after several generations, of one's particular heritage and the generic American traits of tolerance, optimism, belief in opportunity—this insistence upon celebrating what could almost be described as a kind of ethnic tribalism is bewildering. Not even the socialists of the 1930s demanded secession from the republic; the revolution they hoped to bring about was a revolution of class, not race.

Yet "opening up the canon," as these efforts to expand the curriculum are called, isn't as radical as it seems. It's a populist, grass-roots phenomenon, American to the core. What could be more democratic than the new *Columbia Literary History of the United States*, which incorporates Chippewa poems and Whitman's *Song of Myself*, Mark Twain and Jay McInerney? It has chapters on African-American literature, Mexican-American literature, Asian-American literature, on immigrant writers of the nineteenth-century and slave narratives of the Civil War. "There isn't just one story of American literature," says Emory Elliott, a professor of English at the University of California at Riverside and the volume's general editor. "Things are wide open."

No group has been more assiduous in the effort to institutionalize new canonical discoveries than the feminists. Gynocriticism, the study of women's literature, has become a flourishing academic field. Catalogues list English department courses entitled "Feminism, Modernism, and Postmodernism," "Shakespeare and Feminism," and "Feminist Theory and the Humanities." Margaret Williams Ferguson of Columbia University teaches a course on "Renaissance Women of Letters"—Christine de Pisan, Mary Sidney, Aphra Behn. "This is just the tip of the iceberg," says Harvard's Marjorie Garber. "These aren't just oddities or curiosities, but major writers."

The feminist enterprise is more than a matter of introducing works by women into the curriculum, or "mainstreaming." Men and women, it is now believed, have different responses to literature. What is needed, says Princeton's Elaine Showalter, is a "defamiliarization of masculinity, a poetics of the Other"—a critical methodology that addresses gender and sexual difference. On campus bulletin boards I saw notices for lectures entitled "Coming Unstrung: Women, Men, Narrative, and Principles of Pleasure," "Men's Reading, Women's Writing: Canon-Formation and the Case of the Eighteenth-Century French Novel," and "Abulia: Crises of Male Desire in Freud, Thomas Mann, and Musil."

For the post-sixties generation, lit crit is like

child-rearing: both sexes share the burden. Lentricchia's work on Wallace Stevens attempts to sort out the poet's attitude toward his own masculinity—to "feminize" his image. At Harvard, Marjorie Garber has just published a book about cross-dressing that discusses Peter Pan, Laurie Anderson, and old movies. "There's a lot of work to be done on cross-dressing," she says.

All these "texts" that are being rediscovered, republished, revalorized—the sermons and spinsters' diaries, the popular fiction of 1850: Are any of them masterpieces? Jane Tompkins makes a case for Susan Warner's *The Wide, Wide World* (reissued in 1986 by The Feminist Press), and it *is* a powerful book. The story of a young woman orphaned and exiled to bullying relatives in Scotland, Warner's novel portrays an experience of physical and spiritual renunciation that was obviously familiar to its nineteenth-century audience. The writing is energetic and vivid, and the humiliations endured by the heroine recall the trials of Lily Bart in Edith Wharton's *The House of Mirth* or Theodore Dreiser's *Sister Carrie*.

But is it literature? Who decides and by what criteria? The discrimination of value that once occupied critics—that was, indeed, the business of critics from Dr. Johnson's *The Lives of the Poets* (1779–81) through the strenuously opinionated works of the British critic F. R. Leavis in the 1940s and 1950s—has become irrelevant. All that stuff that critics used to talk about, themes of love and death and heroism—forget it. There are no universals, Tompkins insists: "It is the context—which eventually includes the work itself—that creates the value its readers 'discover' there."

What the Duke critics discovered was "the historicization of value," says Stanley Fish. It's not that texts have no literal meaning, as the deconstructors who dominated literary studies in the 1970s believed; they have "an infinite plurality of meanings." The only way to interpret a literary work is to acknowledge the vantage from which we perform the act of interpretation—where we're coming from.

Barbara Herrnstein Smith, a specialist in matters canonical, has written the definitive text on value relativity. *Contingencies of Value* is an exasperating book, especially the first chapter, where Smith clues us in about her life as a professor and claims to be so close to Shakespeare's sonnets that "there have been times when I believed that I had written them myself." Yet for all her confessional posturing, her monstrous immodesty, Smith is on to something. What is taste? What do we experience when we contemplate a work of art? Like Fish, Smith is less interested in the status of a given work than in how that status is established. Who decides what's in and what's out? Those who possess "cultural power." What is art? Whatever the literary establishment says it is.

Smith's book is, among other things, a shrewd polemic against "high-culture critics" intent upon "epistemic self-stabilization" (that is to say, maintaining the status quo). What's wrong with high culture? It's elitist, hierarchical. The new vanguard, Smith asserts, is a tribe of "nonacculturated intellectuals," "postmodern cosmopolites," "exotic visitors and immigrants." In other words, Smith and her colleagues on the academic left.

This hip new professoriate has transformed the landscape of contemporary literature. Many of its members are tenured; they publish books. So why do they cultivate an image of themselves as literary outlaws? Frank Lentricchia isn't the only heavy academic dude around. D. A. Miller, a professor of comparative literature at Berkeley, adorns his books with a photograph that mimes Lentricchia's notorious pose on the back of *Criticism and Social Change*—biceps rippling, arms folded across his chest like Mr. Clean.

One of Lentricchia's recent books is entitled *Ariel and the Police*. Miller is the author of a book entitled *The Novel and the Police*. Both are ostensibly works of literary criticism—Lentricchia is writing largely about William James and Michel Foucault; Miller, about the Victorian novel—but their real subject is the repressive nature of society, power and the containment of power, how our culture "polices" us. "Where are the police in *Barchester Towers*?" Miller asks in a chapter on Trollope. Where, indeed? They're "literally nowhere to be found." No matter. Their very absence is significant, Miller claims, proof that Victorian England was a repressed society. The novel, then, is a form of concealment as well as of disclosure. Its truths are latent, murky, undeclared. Miller's aim as a critic is to "bring literature out of the classroom and into the closet."

What's going on here? Reading between the lines, one begins to get the message. The questioning of authority that's such a pervasive theme in criticism today is a theoretical version of battles that were fought on campuses in the sixties—with real police. "The new epistemology—structuralism, deconstruction—provided the interpretive framework for challenging the canon," says Tompkins. "It's out in the hinterlands now. It's everywhere."

Four

The Decline
of Literary
Criticism

F or an older generation of professors, the transformation of their profession into a battleground of
gender, class, and ideology has been a disaster. The
teaching of literature, objects R.W.B. Lewis, the biographer of Edith Wharton and professor emeritus of
English at Yale, is now a matter of "politics with the
history left out and, indeed, politics with the literature
left out." But of course it's not just politics that Lewis
and his venerable colleagues abhor; it's the *kind* of
politics. From their perspective, opening up the canon

is nothing less than an intellectual counterinsurgency movement—a cover for smuggling into the classroom the countercultural agenda of the 1960s. Once bastions of high culture, the universities now dabble in what Hilton Kramer refers to as "the trash of popular culture."

All this talk of expanding the curriculum, allowing new voices to be heard and acknowledging the importance of other cultures in the shaping of our own, is really an excuse for laissez-faire education, say the traditionalists—the curricular version of "do your own thing." Make no mistake about it, warns Kramer: the politicization of literary studies, the blurring of distinctions between pop culture and high culture, is no mere squabble among professors. "It is our civilization that we believe to be at stake in this struggle," Kramer declared in the *New Criterion*. "The defense of art must not, in other words, be looked upon as a luxury of civilization—to be indulged in and supported when all else is serene and unchallenged—but as the very essence of our civilization."

Politics—the advocacy of a specific ideological cause—is, and always has been, the enemy of art. In the 1930s, the demand for Socialist Realism in Russia—explicit depiction of the class struggle, "correct" art—silenced a whole generation of Soviet writers. Bureaucrats in the Writers' Union determined what got published, while Osip Mandelstam, who made the mistake of writing a satirical poem about Stalin, perished in a Siberian labor camp. Kramer sees the same thing happening now: a cadre of professors, academic *apparatchiks*, has once again appropriated the humanities for its own ideological purposes. The proliferation of ethnic, racial, and gender studies represents "the transformation of art into social science." Ignoring the work of art as *art*, scholars concentrate exclusively on the political and economic conditions that produced it. To reduce art to such narrow preoccupations, Kramer insists, is to deny the transcendent, universal values that give it meaning—to install in the domain of imagination a totalitarian regime:

> So advanced and widespread is this surrender of the arts and the humanities to the social sciences—and to the radical political agenda of the social sciences—that we now have reason, I believe, to look upon the social sciences as a kind of academic gulag to which, on one campus after another and in one learned journal after another, the arts and the sciences have been sent for what, in other parts of the world, it is customary to describe as "reeducation" or "rehabilitation"—in other words, brainwashing.

The rhetoric may be exaggerated, but the situation is much as Kramer describes it. The radicalization of the humanities is an accomplished fact. The recent five-volume Cambridge *New History of American Literature*, edited by Sacvan Bercovitch, a professor of English and American literature at Harvard, provides clear evidence of this radical transformation. Professor Bercovitch's contributors aren't members of the old guard, he explains in a preliminary essay describing the project, but "Americans trained in the sixties and early seventies, spokespersons for 'dissensus.'" For the New Americanists, as the critic Frederick Crews has labeled this generation of scholars, it's not only the curriculum that is undergoing renovation, but who's in charge of it. "The New Americanist program," writes Crews, "aims at altering the literary departments' social makeup as well their dominant style of criticism."

In the last decade, the progenitors of English studies have produced a whole new critical vocabulary. After the politics of gender, the "feminization" of literature, and the assault on the canon, English departments have moved on to "social constructionism," which teaches that literature can be understood only in terms of power—who had it and who didn't. Mark Twain, for instance, is no longer seen as the wise, acerbic humorist revered by generations of readers, according to the Twain scholar Susan Gillman, but as "a deeply historicized writer" whose "most apparently unique and idiosyncratic representations of problematic identity engage with late-nineteenth-century efforts to classify human behavior within biological, sexual, racial, and psychological parameters." Twain's books offer clues to the power relationships that defined nineteenth-century America. He was, despite himself, a representative man.

This trend toward "historicizing" and "ideologizing" works of literature has become institutionalized in our universities. One need only glance over the 1988–89 reading list for one of Stanford's new "Culture, Ideas, Values" survey courses to see which way the wind is blowing. There, among a few survivors from the precanonical era—the Bible, Aeschylus, and Shakespeare—one finds *With His Pistol in His Hand* by Americo Paredes, *He Who Does Evil Should Expect No Good* by Juana Manuela Gorritti, and something called "Documents From the Tupac Amani Rebellion." The presence of such a reading list on a campus known for its conservative approach to the humanities makes it hard to dismiss as paranoia Hilton Kramer's contention that universities are now firmly in the hands of the radical left.

In itself, the politicization of the university is hardly a new phenomenon. The era from 1945 to 1960, generally thought to have been quiescent—the Eisenhower years, the tranquilized fifties—was in fact "a period of constantly growing political commitment, political zeal, and political ideology," wrote Robert Nisbet in his classic book about American education in the postwar era, *The Degradation of the Academic Dogma*. The hostile attention that Senator Joseph McCarthy trained on leftwing professors during the 1950s served to radicalize them in self-defense.

What distinguishes academic politics now from academic politics then? Politicization—I employ these unwieldy words with the greatest reluctance—has been accompanied by professionalization. The ex-radicals in college English departments aren't motivated to write the way they do out of a determination to overthrow the United States government; it's become the approved way of finding something new to say about old books. In 1987, according to the *New*

York Times education reporter Edward B. Fiske, scholarly journals published 215 articles on Milton, 132 on Henry James, and 554 on Shakespeare. How can an associate professor, up for tenure, find anything new to say about these authors? It isn't easy. Thus the trend described by Northwestern professor Lawrence Lipking as "competitive reading"—the quest for innovative interpretations, for "the reading that curves or swerves, like a grading curve. The further the student advances, the more curves are needed, until finally, in graduate school, the choice of reading differs so much from the texts most other people have read, or the interpretation differs so much from earlier interpretations, that it becomes publishable."

I offer, in support of Professor Lipking's thesis, a recent essay published in the *Yale Journal of Criticism* entitled "Auto-canonization: Tropes of Self-Legitimation in 'Popular Culture.'" This essay, by Jonathan Freedman, a professor of English at Yale, examines the social implications of the curriculum debate and speculates about the consequences of opening up the canon. Interpreting, in the approved deconstructionist fashion, a song by Barry Manilow entitled "I Write the Songs," Professor Freedman asserts that the "I" of the song is a highly problematic figure whose identity depends on two crucial assumptions:

> ... first, that the songs are written not in the Derridean sense of the written as the arbitrary or the impersonal but rather in the older sense of the written as composed, as

organized by a primary, fully individuated consciousness exercising itself in acts of spontaneous but disciplined creativity; and second, that this consciousness, this "I" that writes the songs, has some sort of social role or function to fulfill in the world at large.

Let me offer another sample, one that reflects a somewhat different but still characteristic methodology. I choose, virtually at random, a sentence from *The Critical Difference: Essays in the Contemporary Rhetoric of Reading* by Barbara Johnson: "In his median position between the Budd/Claggart opposition and the acceptance/irony opposition, Captain Vere functions as a focus for the conversion of polarity into ambiguity and back again." The discussion is of Melville's *Billy Budd;* the author teaches in the departments of French and comparative literature at Harvard. As a sentence, it's no better or worse than many thousands like it, and it's certainly no more obscure; to someone trained in the language of contemporary criticism, it does indeed yield a meaning. Captain Vere is a *reader*, stresses Professor Johnson; which isn't to say that he reads books, but rather that he is the character who represents Melville's own authorial point of view. But of course we can't ascribe a particular interpretation to Vere/Melville's "reading" of events; interpretation, remember, is an activity fraught with variables. The "reader's" point of view is inherently unstable; to criticize a work of art is to assess our ignorance—in effect, to question the whole enterprise.

Does criticism have to be written this way? There are plenty of critics around—especially critics of an older generation—who are willing to put their readings on the line. The distinguished Harold Bloom of Yale, for one—however intricate his own critical vocabulary—has never been shy about saying what a poem or novel means. But the critical method practiced by Freedman and Johnson dominates the scene, and it has a trickle-down effect. When students do read, complains William Pritchard, a professor of English at Amherst and one of the few critics around who writes for a general audience, they're more likely to have read the French deconstructionist Jacques Derrida on Rousseau or Roland Barthes on Balzac than Rousseau or Balzac. They become adept at a kind of academic discourse learned from their professors, who spend their time discussing "what XY recently wrote about *Jane Eyre* in the last issue of *Diacritics* or *Signs.*"

This is how it's done now. The civilizing purpose of literature, its capacity to inculcate values even as it instructs us in the ambiguity of human conduct, is disparaged or ignored. "The best citizen," claimed Lionel Trilling, "is the person who has learned from the great minds and souls of the past how beautiful reason and virtue are and how difficult to attain." How archaic those words sound! They reflect a humility that's vanished from the scene. The critic is the artist. Literary criticism has become an elaborate game of interpretation. As a disenchanted professor quoted in Lynne Cheney's report puts it, "The level of specialization increases, while the significance of research moves toward the vanishing point."

Academic pedantry is nothing new. The late Edmund Wilson, in his famous attack on the Modern Language Association and its methods, "The Fruits of the MLA," produced a masterpiece of satirical muckraking. Perusing the program of the association's 1968 convention, Wilson was greatly amused by the announced topics, among them "Flowers, Women, and Song in the Poetry of William Carlos Williams" and "The Unity of George Peele's *The Old Wives' Tale*"—topics that seem straightforward compared with the elaborate titles of today. Of course, these seminars weren't meant to appeal to a general audience, Wilson concluded, "but to serve as offered self-qualifications in what is really an employment agency" (same as now). As for the "definitive editions" that so many MLA scholars labored over, huge volumes laden with textual commentary about variant spellings and other equally weighty matters, Wilson marveled at the sheer expenditure of energy: texts were submitted to the scrutiny of a device known as the Hinman Collating Machine, which registered discrepancies in drafts; professional proofreaders read them backwards in order to discover typos without being distracted by the words' sense. Apropos the official edition of Melville's *Typee,* Wilson reported, quoting from its preface: "And then there is the great hyphenation problem: 'The missing hyphen in *married* at E213-2 (191.34) is also obvious, since the word is not a compound.'"

Things were no better when I attended the MLA's 1986 convention, which featured hundreds upon hundreds of conferences devoted to such topics as "Eddie and May's Old Man: Theatricality in Sam

Shepard's *Fool for Love*," "Hannah Cooks the Tur-
key: Woody Allen's Accommodations of Postmodern
Irony," "The Repressions of Psychoanalysis: Lesbi-
ans, Mothers, and Others in Literature and Theory,"
and many, many more. Literature wasn't the only
subject on the agenda: attention was also paid to the
so-called real world. You could attend workshops on
the travails of part-time teaching ("Out of the Bus and
Into the Bullpen: The Adjunct Life at Queens"),
on "The Impact of Homo- and Lesbophobia on
Academic Careers," on "Pragmatic Dissonance in
Greeting-Card Humor," on *Bright Lights, Big City,*
Back to the 'Burbs: Jay McInerney's Encounter With
the Other." One of my journalistic colleagues on the
MLA beat described the conference as an exercise in
"breaking down constituencies by gender and body
size." (Sure enough, there was a session entitled
"Seizing Power: Gender, Representation, and Body
Scale.")

Four years later, Roger Kimball penetrated behind the lines. It was clear from his report, "The Pe-
riphery v. The Center: The MLA in Chicago" (a title
that deliberately emulated the obligatory hyphenated
titles of MLA papers), that the rhetorical heat had
been turned up. "How, specifically, do the multicul-
turalist imperatives of political correctness manifest
themselves in the subjects addressed at a major academic conference on literature?" Kimball asked, writing in the *New Criterion.* "For one thing, literature
itself takes a distant back seat to a wide variety of
currently fashionable ideological concerns." There
were panels at the 1990 conference on "Revolting

Acts: Gay Performance in the Sixties," "The Racial Politics of Intertextuality: Gloria Naylor's Deconstruction of Shakespeare," and "The Poetics of 'Othering': Gender, Class, and Cultural Identity in the Literature of Africa and its Diaspora." Some of the conference papers seemed willfully lurid (for instance, "Mapping the Frontier of the Black Hole: Toward a Black Feminist Theory" and "The Lesbian Phallus: Or, Does Heterosexuality Exist?"); they were designed, noted Kimball, to have a prurient appeal. In any event, the drift was clear. The proper subject of literary studies was no longer literature, but politics. "The effect is not to make one more politically 'sensitive,' " as Kimball forcefully put it, "but to transform a concern with literature into an obsession with one's race, one's sex, one's sexual preferences, one's ethnic origin."

As a rule, I'm suspicious of literary journalists who put down academics. I suspect my colleagues of the ambivalence I feel myself—envy of the pastoral surroundings in which English professors get to work, their job security, their summer vacations, the time they spend among books—and impatience with their hermetic approach to the literary vocation. And there's something hypocritical about the self-righteous thundering of the neoconservatives, whose own rhetoric is itself so obviously political in its intent, the yearning for a past that never was. (Gerald Graff calls it "educational fundamentalism.") But professors themselves attest to the decline of purposeful scholarship within their ranks. "To anyone who pays attention to current controversies," writes Lawrence

Lipking of Northwestern, "nothing could be plainer than that most of the disputants have not read the works that the others are proposing." Professor Graff, who has been urging his colleagues to "teach the debate," is equally blunt. "At the very moment when external forces have conspired to deflate the importance and truth of literature, literary theory delivers the final blow itself." Or consider this remarkable bit of testimony:

> English and literary studies have reached a point in their theoretical development when they've become almost incapable of communicating to the layman at the very historical moment when they've most needed to justify their existence. The brightest and most innovative people in literary criticism are as impenetrable as nuclear physicists. The left-wing intelligentsia is trapped in a kind of ghetto that only they understand, and so can't bring any leverage to bear on the body politic.

The writer is David Lodge, a well-known English novelist and, until a few years ago, a professor of modern English literature at the University of Birmingham. (He is also the editor of a collection of essays on deconstructionism.) The situation he deplores in England is virtually identical to the situation here.

Academics have been notably reticent in the face of all this criticism. The one official response that got any attention was a pamphlet issued by the American

Council of Learned Societies (ACLS). Instigated as a reply to Lynne Cheney's report, *Humanities in America*, ACLS Occasional Paper No. 7 attempts to rebut the charges leveled against English professors and their kind—a defense of academic theory and practice. Entitled "Speaking for the Humanities," No. 7 is a collaborative enterprise, signed by six professors whose efforts were coordinated by Professor George Levine of Rutgers University. Their intent was to answer attacks on the state of learning in the universities, "for those attacks have practical consequences that will affect the future development, not only of the humanities, but of society as well."

Canon-busting is in the ascendant, contend the authors of "Speaking for the Humanities," so there must be something to it: "Much of what most matters in modern thought challenges claims to universality and subverts traditional assumptions of authority." And since it's in the ascendant, the New Canonists— to coin a term—are merely doing their duty. They pride themselves on being "professionals rather than amateurs—belletrists who unself-consciously sustain traditional hierarchies, traditional social and cultural exclusions, assuming that their audience is both universal and homogenous." I translate: Those who endorse a core curriculum, a canon of great works, are old-fashioned. To claim that such a canon exists is to discriminate against the literature of minorities. To teach this canon is to ignore the ethnic diversity of college students in the 1990s. Specialization is a necessary aspect of *professionalization;* it enables professors to develop alternative canons, to challenge the

status quo. And that is a good thing: "For professionalization makes thought possible by developing sets of
questions, imposing norms which have then to be
questioned and thereby promoting debate on key
problems." *Professionalization makes thought possible.* As Gertrude Stein once said, "Interesting if true."

Is the situation really so dire? In fact, contend the
authors of ACLS Paper No. 7, what we are witnessing
is a revival of the humanities. The statistics invoked by
Cheney are inconclusive, they assert; in many universities, the number of students enrolled in English and
history majors is up. They point approvingly to "the
proliferation of interdisciplinary humanities centers"
dedicated to the promotion of learning in a wide variety of fields, from philosophy to psychoanalysis. And if
the humanities *are* in trouble, they stress, it's not entirely the humanists' fault. There has always been a
virulent strain of philistinism in American life.
Cheney's broadside is merely the latest symptom of it:

> United States society, with a tradition of
> anti-intellectualism and interest in science,
> engineering, economics, has been finding it
> convenient to indict the humanities for their
> intellectual weaknesses in attempting to en-
> gage practical moral and social issues; they
> have, so the charge goes, lapsed from the
> Arnoldian ideals of seeing the object as it
> really is and learning the best that has been
> thought and said. Instead, they allegedly
> pander to new interest groups and mix the
> universal ideals of art and morality with his-

tory, politics, gender, and race. Thus, alarming changes that are surely primarily connected to national and international restructuring of political and economic power are partly attributed to the failure of the humanities to think unmixedly and speak unequivocally for the universal values in the Western traditions of art, literature, and philosophy.

How does this "restructuring of political and economic power" affect the humanities? George Levine, chief editor of the ACLS paper, has an explanation: "While campus interest in the humanities declined, the United States began to doubt that it was still the leading economic power of the world," he wrote in a recent issue of *Raritan*, a quarterly journal associated with Rutgers University. "At the same time, middle-class students began to wonder if they could expect to achieve the economic status of their own parents." In other words, the humanities are a luxury to be dispensed with in belt-tightening times. Students are no longer willing to make the sacrifices necessary for a career in higher learning. If becoming an English professor means forfeiting our inalienable right to a two-car garage, who needs it?

Whether the oil crisis of 1973 will prove to have been partially responsible for the declining enrollment in the humanities, as Professor Levine maintains, is a highly debatable proposition. One could just as easily argue that the arts and humanities prosper in unprosperous times, that economic recessions promote the kind of holiday from materialistic ambition that memoirists of the 1930s and 1940s remember so fondly. For many writers and intellectuals, the Depression was a liberating time, a time of freedom. "No longer chained to the wheel of career and profession," the philosopher William Barrett recalled in his memoir, *The Truants,* "we could abandon ourselves to the delight of irrelevant studies."

Those days, of course, are long gone. Barrett's vision of the good life—idling away afternoons on a bench in Washington Square with the latest issue of *Partisan Review*—is archaic, quaint. Ours is an increasingly nonverbal culture, a culture in which books no longer possess the aura of sanctity they once did. The ecstatic literary apprenticeship that Alfred Kazin, our foremost critic, so rapturously evoked in his classic memoir, *A Walker in the City,* of entering the Brownsville Public Library on a summer's evening and "trembling in front of the shelves," isn't an experience likely to find its way into the memoirs of my generation. Reminiscing in the *New Republic*'s seventy-fifth-anniversary issue about his career as a man of letters, Kazin supplied a memorable epitaph: "Our literary period may yet be remembered as one in which the book business replaced the literary world, in which literary theory replaced literature, and in which, as Irving Howe has said, Marxism came to its end—in the English Department."

The 1960s and its legacy isn't wholly to blame. The idea of the university as a place where independent scholarship could flourish was threatened long before the attack on the canon. Its demise can be dated back to the postwar era. Until then, the universities' mandate was assumed—"that it is good for students to read Chaucer, Jane Austen, T. S. Eliot, good to study history, philosophy, sociology, and physics, good to accumulate knowledge in the learned disciplines, each of these good in and for itself," as Robert Nisbet put it in *The Degradation of the Academic Dogma*. In the 1940s, a new phenomenon was visited upon the academic community—what Nisbet variously calls "the higher capitalism," "the new capitalism," and "academic capitalism." The universities were invaded by government and private foundations. Suddenly the big money was in research. Institutes, centers, and bureaus sprang up on campuses across the land. "For the first time in Western history, professors and scholars were thrust into the unwonted position of entrepreneurs in incessant search for new sources of capital, of new revenue, and, taking the word in its larger sense, of profits." Universities became bureaucratic institutions. Professors became captains of intellectual industry. The humanities became irrelevant.

The response to this unplanned and undesired obsolescence has been to professionalize the humanities, to make them emulate what are perceived to be more objective, *scientific* disciplines like anthropology, linguistics, sociology. The absurdly complex language of much contemporary literary criticism is an effort, I suspect, to mime these disciplines; it confers a spurious authority on judgments and procedures that are subjective by their very nature—are *supposed to be* subjective. (What was exhilarating about the liter-

ary essays of F. R. Leavis, who established his own
canon and imposed it upon generations of grateful
Cambridge undergraduates, was the sense of personal
authority it conveyed; by the "pursuit of true judgment," of course, Leavis meant his own judgment, but
he argued so forcefully on its behalf that he made
criticism seem objective.) Rather than defend the idea
of the university as a place where undergraduates are
encouraged to pursue knowledge for its own sake,
humanities departments have made a profession out
of repudiating their own claims to intellectual authority. The consequence of this curious self-betrayal, as
the critic Louis Menand has argued, is to cancel out
their own *raison d'etre*:

> Contemporary critical theory—in particular
> post-structuralist theories, emphasizing the
> indeterminacy of meaning, and ideological
> theories, emphasizing the social construction
> of values—rejects precisely the belief on
> which the professional apparatus of the uni-
> versity (graduate exams, dissertation de-
> fenses, tenure review, publication in refer-
> eed journals, and so forth) depends: the
> belief that the pursuit of knowledge is a dis-
> interested activity whose results can be eval-
> uated objectively by other trained specialists
> in one's field.

What does contemporary critical theory say?
That culture is a myth, a tool for establishing hierarchies of value—in effect, an instrument of oppression,

its primary agent of domination "a hegemonic, homo-erotic/homophobic male canon of cultural mastery and coercive erotic double binding," to quote Eve Kosofsky Sedgwick, a professor of English at Duke. Given the prevalence of this belief, it's not only futile to demand that students master a core of classics, it's hypocritical. If their professors don't believe in the canon, why should they?

Say we assume the worst: that innovations in the curriculum have politicized the humanities, that the proliferation of courses in Third World literature, of deconstructionist and feminist criticism, represents—I quote from Roger Kimball's widely discussed book, *Tenured Radicals: How Politics Has Corrupted Our Higher Education*—"an ideologically motivated assault on the intellectual and moral substance of our culture." Even if what Kimball says its true, even if there *is* a crisis in higher education, why is it a matter of public concern? So universities are going through a troubled phase: what impact does that have on the more immediate crisis—the deterioration of our inner-city schools?

It matters because values, conduct, and the prevailing moral tone are established at the top. "One way or another," writes Chester Finn, the former assistant secretary of education, "every significant development in higher education eventually echoes in the elementary-secondary system." Higher education sets the national agenda.

In the case of curriculum reform, it has already happened. The college boards in history now offer questions on child-rearing practices and the place of women in society. A sample: "How and why did the lives and status of northern middle-class women change between 1776 and 1876?" It's not a bad question, actually; but how many seventeen-year-olds are prepared to answer it? Never mind. The Committee of Examiners in Advanced Placement (AP) History "believed the AP program should be on the cutting edge of curricular reform," reports the historian Gertrude Himmelfarb, "and this view eventually prevailed."

The new history, like the new literary criticism, is no mere fad, stresses Himmelfarb; it's closer to "a revolution in the discipline." And the consequences of this revolution are widely felt. "The examinations send out signals to high schools throughout the country telling them what kind of history should be taught if their students are to compete successfully for admission to college," writes Himmelfarb; in effect, they "establish something very like a national curriculum."

For confirmation, one need only consult a remarkable document entitled "One Nation, Many Peoples: A Declaration of Cultural Interdependence." This controversial report, the product of a task force appointed by Thomas Sobol, the New York State commissioner of education, addressed the issue of how well the state's elementary and high school systems were responding to the needs of minority groups. Textbooks, the task force found, are dominated by a "Eurocentric conceptualization and modality" that emphasizes the dominance of whites. Members of minority cultures—African-Americans,

Asian-Americans, Latinos, and Native Americans—learn from these textbooks to feel "alienated and devalued," while "members of the majority culture are exclusionary and overvalued." What the high school curriculum fails to teach, according to the Sobol report, is that the deck is stacked: our two-party system, Congress, and the president's cabinet are "effective vehicles for articulating and aggregating the interests of the rich and powerful, the true benefactors of the 'new Anglo-Saxon model.'" The report's chief architect is Leonard Jeffries, Jr.

The Sobol report elicited some harsh criticism. Diane Ravitch noted that the eleventh-grade syllabus described "the two major influences on the United States Constitution as the European Enlightenment and the political system of the Iroquois confederacy"—a unique interpretation of American history, to say the least. Like it or not, pointed out the political scientist Andrew Hacker, "for almost all of this nation's history the major decisions have been made by white Christian men."

Unmoved by these objections, the Board of Regents voted in July 1991 to adopt the findings of the Sobol report, and the drafting of a new curriculum for New York City public schools is under way. Instead of reading about "Orientals" or "slaves," students in the public high schools of New York will read about "Asians" and "enslaved persons." The story of the early colonization of the United States will be revised to take into account "the long-established Hispanic influence on settlements in the West." The meaning of Thanksgiving and Columbus Day will be taught with special attention to the disregard those holidays show for "indigenous peoples."

Fair enough. But the Sobol report went a good deal further, shifting the emphasis from "the mastery of information to the development of fundamental tools, concepts, and intellectual processes that make people learners who can approach knowledge in a variety of ways and struggle with the contradictions." From now on, it won't be enough to know the capital of Idaho or who Pocahantas was; seventh-graders will be expected to know why they should know these facts and not others: "The subject matter content should be *treated as socially constructed* and therefore tentative—as is all knowledge." Deconstructionism comes to P.S. 87.

Five

Cultural Illiteracy

At first glance, E. D. Hirsch's *Cultural Literacy* seemed as unlikely a bestseller as *The Closing of the American Mind*. Originally a lecture given before the Modern Language Association, it was published as an essay in the *American Scholar* in 1983. "I received a letter from Robert Payton, president of the Exxon Education Foundation," Hirsch wrote in the introduction to his book, "encouraging me to start acting on my perceptions rather than just writing them down."

Spurred on by an Exxon grant, Hirsch began to compile his now-famous list of the "items" that, if known and mastered, would enable this and future generations of students to attain cultural literacy. In 1987 he published his book, which instantly made the bestseller list; for forty weeks it was second only to Bloom's. The paperback has sold 600,000 copies. Hirsch, a professor of English at the University of Virginia and a scholar of eighteenth-century literature, has become the latest representative of that new American type, the academic celebrity.

What is cultural literacy? The answer is simply put in the subtitle of Hirsch's book: *What Every American Needs to Know*. By "culture" Hirsch doesn't mean "high culture," but "basic information," the names and events that enable us to decipher the world. In order to function in society, to work and to communicate, he argues, people need to possess a certain number of facts about their own history. The key events in our past, the key phrases in our literature, are in themselves a kind of language, a code that educated people decipher in their daily lives without even knowing it. Hirsch reminisces about his father, an old-fashioned businessman who used to quote Shakespeare in his correspondence and often used the phrase "There is a tide"—shorthand for "There is a tide in the affairs of men / Which taken at the flood leads on to fortune" from *Julius Caesar*—to illustrate how one knows intuitively when to buy or sell. "To persuade somebody that your recommendation is wise and well founded, you have to give lots of reasons and cite known examples and authorities," wrote

Hirsch. "My father accomplished that and more in four words, which made quoting Shakespeare as effective as any efficiency consultant could wish."

For Allan Bloom, the decline of educational standards can be traced to the decline of philosophy (a word he uses to mean the humanities in general); to ignore the classics is ultimately to weaken the very foundations of our society. Hirsch is more pragmatic. For him, the purpose of education isn't to produce a handful of Greek scholars who can preserve the great intellectual traditions of the West, as Bloom would have it, but to prepare us for the complex social transactions of everyday life. It's not a nation of English professors that Hirsch aspires to create, but a nation in which ordinary people are literate enough to negotiate effectively in the world. "High stakes," he writes, are involved in the curriculum debate:

> . . . breaking the cycle of illiteracy for deprived children; raising the living standard of families who have been illiterate; making our country more competitive in international markets; achieving greater social justice; enabling all citizens to participate in the political process; bringing us closer to the Ciceronian ideal of universal public discourse—in short, achieving fundamental goals of the founders at the birth of the republic.

There's nothing abstract about this imperative. Behind Hirsch's high-minded rhetoric is a pretty straightforward message: You can't expect people to grasp the basic principles of democracy unless they know what those principles are. And you can't expect them to function effectively in the world unless they're literate.

Hirsch's book was notably even-tempered and unpolemical; he sounded like a guy who was trying to help. And he had actually *done* something. He had gone around speaking before state boards of education; he had founded a Cultural Literacy Foundation, publishing a newsletter and circulating to schools around the country a provisional list of what students at every grade level ought to know; he had produced a *Dictionary of Cultural Literacy* and a six-volume textbook (still in the works) designed to teach the rudiments of American history, the major works of English and American literature, and the natural sciences. But in academic circles, *Cultural Literacy* kindled almost as much fury as *The Closing of the American Mind*. At a conference on "Liberal Arts Education in the Late Twentieth Century" held at Duke University in 1988, Barbara Herrnstein Smith rose and delivered a vitriolic diatribe, "Cult-Lit: Hirsch, Literacy, and the 'National Culture,'" that enumerated in harsh language the magnitude of Hirsch's sins. What did he mean by *shared culture?* Smith wanted to know. There was no such thing, and any efforts to define one represented, in Smith's words, "context-specific, pragmatically adjusted negotiations of (and through) *difference.*" Hirsch was trying to homogenize and oppress minorities by making them conform to *his* idea of culture. Nor did Smith have a whole lot of sympathy

for Hirsch's idealized vision of what our nation is all about. "Wild applause; fireworks; music," she noted with heavy sarcasm after quoting his invocation to the "fundamental goals" of the Founding Fathers: *"America the Beautiful;* all together, now: *Calvin Coolidge, Gunga Din, Peter Pan, spontaneous combustion.* Hurrah for America and the national culture! Hurrah!"

Okay, so there are flaws in Hirsch's argument: his definition of a "literate national culture" is vague; his list of "What Every American Needs to Know" is biased. But his basic indictment—that we're in the midst of a crisis with long-range social consequences—seems to me beyond dispute. Americans know less than ever. In a 1988 survey of high school students' scientific achievement level prepared by the International Association for the Evaluation of Educational Achievement, the United States ranked third-to-last out of fifteen developed nations; in a 1970 survey, the U.S. had ranked seventh. It's not that other nations have improved in terms of education; we have deteriorated. U.S. Scholastic Aptitude Test (SAT) scores have declined precipitously over the last decade: from 1972 to 1984, 56 percent fewer students scored over 600 and 73 percent fewer scored over 650. A 1983 report by the National Commission on Excellence in Education stated, "For the first time in the history of our country, the educational skills of one generation will not surpass, will not equal, will not even approach those of their parents."

Hirsch's book is full of frightening statistics: Two-thirds of seventeen-year-olds weren't aware that

the Civil War occurred between 1850 and 1900. Nearly half couldn't identify Stalin; nearly one-fourth couldn't identify Churchill. When Hirsch's son, a high school Latin teacher, asked his class to name an epic poem by Homer, one student volunteered "The Alamo?" Another, informed that Latin was no longer spoken, asked, "What do they speak in Latin America?" At a conference of college deans, Hirsch reported in the *New York Review of Books,* he was regaled with "a chorus of anecdotes" about the decline in literacy among entering freshmen: "To these administrators, the debate over Stanford University's required courses seemed interesting but less than momentous when compared with the problem of preparing students to participate intelligently in any university-level curriculum."

It's just as much a problem in the Ivy League as anywhere else. Jerry Doolittle, an English instructor at Harvard, designed a quiz for his freshmen students to determine their level of literacy. They were given twenty statements and asked to fill in the blanks. Among the sample questions were the following:

I think that I shall never see a poem _____ (four words)

Quoth the raven, _____ (one word)

A jug of wine, a loaf of bread and _____ (one word)

The average score was seven out of twenty—a figure somewhat inflated, Doolittle confessed, by two statements that everyone in the class completed correctly:

"Winston tastes good, like a _____" (two words) and "This Bud's for _____" (one word). And this was Harvard!

According to Richard Marius, director of Harvard's Expository Writing Program, arriving freshmen are so woefully deficient in the basic skills of reading and writing that a remedial course is required just to get them to the point where their peers would have been a generation ago. "This generation does not read," Marius laments in *Teaching Literature: What Is Needed Now*. They're unfamiliar with the Bible, Shakespeare, Milton; they don't even know the Gettysburg Address: "They are strangers not only to those points of reference that might help them navigate the literary sea, but also to the underlying cadences that have governed the development of written English. They cannot write because they have not read and they cannot hear."

The poet and essayist Katha Pollitt offers telling corroborative evidence. In her modern poetry seminar at Barnard, Pollitt reports, none of her students had even a bare familiarity with any poems published more than a decade ago. "Robert Lowell was as far outside their frame of reference as Alexander Pope." They didn't see how a knowledge of earlier poetry was necessary to their work; in fact, they found the work of earlier poets discouraging, for it showed up their own deficiencies. A new way to deal with the potentially smothering effects of one's precursors: Don't have any.

One could argue that our indifference to literature—and to literacy—is a function of our distracted

culture, but a contributing factor, I suspect, is the virtual abolition of requirements that so many colleges embraced in the late sixties and seventies (a development that quickly replicated itself in public secondary schools). It's all very well to talk of the character-building sustenance that books provide, but most people don't read unless they're compelled to; and higher education was designed to serve that purpose. School once was, "and might frankly *be*," Pollitt reminds us, "the place where one read the books that are a little off-putting, that have gone a little cold, that you might overlook because they do not address, in reader-friendly contemporary fashion, the issues most immediately at stake in modern life but that, with a little study, turn out to have a great deal to say."

In the 1980s, a reaction set in to the *laissez-faire* education that characterized my college days, and a number of colleges moved to reinstate some semblance of a core. (Some had never abandoned it: the Great Books course instituted at Columbia after World War I survives in recognizable form to this day.) At Harvard, where the general education program—created to provide students with "the common knowledge and the common values on which a free society depends"—had fallen into disrepair, a core curriculum was once again proposed, and a task force was convened to consider the matter. It found in favor of establishing such a curriculum, but weaseled out of actually trying to impose one. What it came up with was a set of courses divided into ten categories—Social Analysis, Moral Reasoning, Foreign Cultures, Literature and Arts, and so on. But the Core's architects,

eager to avoid the charge of ethno- or Eurocentricism, threw in a potpourri of courses from other disciplines and fields: "Building the Shogun's Realm: The Unification of Japan (1560–1650)"; "Caribbean Societies: Socioeconomic Change and Cultural Adaptations"; "Individual, Community, and Nation in Japan." Since you only have to choose one course from each area, it's possible to graduate, notes Caleb Nelson in a strongly argued condemnation of "Harvard's Hollow 'Core,' " without ever having read any nineteenth-century British novels; without having read Virgil, Milton, or Dostoyevsky; without having taken a course on the Enlightenment or the Renaissance or the American Civil War. One section leader editorialized in the *Crimson:* "Most Harvard students taking Core courses are no more likely to have read and seriously understood the philosophical, political, or cultural foundations of their own United States than if they selected thirty-two random courses from the catalogue."

But that was never the Core's intent. "There are simply too many facts, too many theories, too many subjects, too many specializations to permit arranging all knowledge into an acceptable hierarchy," reasoned its founders. Better to concentrate on methodology. And so they did. The Harvard Core—I quote from the 1991–92 catalogue—

> does not define intellectual breadth as the mastery of a set of Great Books, or the digestion of a specific quantum of information, or the surveying of current knowledge in cer-

tain fields. Rather, the Core seeks to introduce students to the major *approaches to knowledge* in areas that the faculty considers indispensable to undergraduate education. It aims to show what kinds of knowledge and what forms of inquiry exist in these areas, how different means of analysis are acquired, how they are used, and what their value is.

How can we master these italicized *approaches to knowledge* if we possess no knowledge to approach? One might well ask . . . But Harvard has abdicated its role in this matter, believing that to choose is to discriminate (in the pejorative sense). The devisers of the Core were even reluctant to name one of the courses in it "Western Civilization," according to Nelson, for fear of offending non-Occidental constituencies. (The course is now called "Western Societies, Politics, and Cultures.")

Ever since the inception of the humanities as a field of academic study, the aim of the university has been to produce generalists familiar with the main outlines of Western civilization. All E.D. Hirsch is asking is that we preserve—or, given the way things are in our schools, relearn—this cultural lexicon. How can we challenge the list, or the idea of a list, if we can't identify the names in dispute? "It is, after all, easier to teach Shakespeare in a Stephen Greenblattish, quasi-Foucauldian way to students who recognize the names of Shakespeare's plays," argues Richard Rorty, "easier to explain possibilities of social transformation

to students who know that the French Revolution antedated the Russian. . . . " Only a theoretical counterinsurgency movement dedicated to the proposition that basic literacy is an ideologically charged issue could object to such a benign construal of Hirsch's thesis.

That movement is now in full cry.

Six

The End of
Tradition

In his classic memoir, *Enemies of Promise*, Cyril Connolly lists the English writers he absorbed as a boy at Eton: "Webster was my favorite Elizabethan, then came Donne, and after him Marvell, Herrick, and Sir Thomas Browne." Connolly read Boswell, Gibbon, and Laurence Sterne; he wallowed in the Romantic poets. It was an education typical of that day and class—it's still typical today. To be literate in England is to be thoroughly acquainted with its literature. The classics of English prose and poetry resonate in the popular imagination. London newspaper columnists quote Macaulay. Politicians and government officials write scholarly books. Noel Annan, the former minister of education, is an authority on the literature of Victorian England. Michael Foot, once head of the Labor Party, has published a creditable biography of Byron.

For England's middle and upper classes, literature is part of their cultural inheritance. It reflects their customs, their speech, their experience of the world—a world that in some crucial respects hasn't changed for centuries. The London of Thackeray, the London of Dickens, isn't all that different from the London of Kingsley (or even Martin) Amis, the celebrated father-and-son team of contemporary British fiction. There is continuity.

The same holds true of France, where writers are public figures, even heroes, and always have been. The novelist André Malraux was de Gaulle's minister of culture. Twenty-five thousand people attended the funeral of Jean-Paul Sartre. The French Academy, composed of forty eminent *hommes de lettres*, is a more august body than its senate. Every *lycéen* knows his way around the Pléiade editions, those handsome, beautifully produced volumes of the French classics printed on thin paper. The national literature and the national identity are one.

Englishness and Frenchness are complex traits, not easily susceptible to definition. They embrace profound differences of class, accent, and background. But they're still recognizable identities; they describe a national type. There is a certain insularity about these cultures, but it's hard for an American not to envy their cozy self-regard. I remember once, walking in the countryside of Cornwall with an English poet who amazed me with his knowledge of local lore. Each stone, each house, each ancient church had its history. Kings had trod this ground.

It's exhausting to be an American—you have to conjure up an identity out of nothing, become self-made. Character is fate. In England, character is also fate, but so is heredity; the visible evidence of tradition enables English citizens to think of themselves as transitory tenants of a nation that is destined to outlast them. Americans are immigrants. We're all from somewhere else. After the Puritans and other dissenting sects came the Scandinavians, the Swiss, the Irish, the Jews of Eastern Europe, the Italians, the Chinese. Since World War II, our borders have been overwhelmed by new hyphenated populations: Asian-Americans, Mexican-Americans, Russian-Americans. Flatbush Avenue in Brooklyn has been colonized by Ethiopians, Trinidadians, Tibetans, and Pakistanis. They're citizens of the United States. Americans? There is no such indigenous type.

Yet we have an American literature. The great nineteenth-century flowering that produced Whitman, Hawthorne, Melville, Emerson, and Thoreau—main figures of what came to be known as the American Renaissance—was evidence that we possessed, if not a national identity, at the very least a culture of our own. "When one looks back at Victorian England and the America of Whitman and Lincoln," writes David Bromwich of Yale in his essay "The Future of

Tradition: Notes on the Crisis in the Humanities,"
"one is impressed by the consensus a majority of the
educated observed in the arts and moral sciences.
Not, indeed, a consensus of judgment, but a consensus
about the grounds of judgment." In politics and sensibility this majority was progressive, liberal, and egalitarian; it was attuned to "the topics of the time,"
wrote Emerson: "the literature of the poor, the feel-
ings of the child, the philosophy of the street, the
meaning of a household life." It shared a set of assumptions and beliefs that, in their aggregate, could
be called American.

Our literature, like our political tradition, is es-
sentially democratic. The great American novelists of
the period between the two world wars—Hemingway
and Fitzgerald, Faulkner and Thomas Wolfe—came
out of the provinces to produce a distinctive American
idiom. Like their nineteenth-century predecessors,
they were radically unalike: their books are a com-
pendium of the American vernacular, from the laconic
Midwestern idiom of Hemingway's Nick Adams stories to the sophisticated New York slang of F. Scott
Fitzgerald, from the backwoods South of Faulkner to
the North Carolina mountain dialect of Wolfe. Yet
they had studied—and were determined to emulate—
the masters of English literature. Faulkner started out
as a poet, writing bad Elizabethan verse. Thomas
Wolfe was inspired by the King James Bible.

The novelists of the postwar generation appren-
ticed themselves to the same literary tradition. English poets like Milton and Coleridge were alien to
Saul Bellow when he was growing up on the North-

west Side of Chicago in a Yiddish-speaking home;
they might as well have been writing in a foreign language. But these were the authors he read in school.
Bellow has a wonderful image in a lecture he once
gave at the Chicago Public Library of an old Swedish
schoolteacher reciting *King Lear* to a roomful of Jewish children whose parents were just off the boat. He
didn't go to the public library to read the Talmud, he's
often noted, but the works of Sherwood Anderson,
Theodore Dreiser, Edgar Lee Masters, and Vachel
Lindsay: "These were people who had resisted the
material weight of American society and who
proved—what was not immediately obvious—that the
life lived in great manufacturing, shipping, and bank-
ing centers, with their slaughter stink, their great
slums, prisons, hospitals, and schools, was also a
human life."

There *was* an America, then—the America that
was in these books. And it was the children of immigrants—writers like Irving Howe, Lionel Trilling, and
Philip Rahv—who would turn out to be among the
most articulate interpreters of English and American
literature in the postwar era. Trilling on Hawthorne,
Howe on Sherwood Anderson, Rahv on Henry James
(a writer whose place in the canon he was instrumen-
tal in restoring): these critics knew their way around
the Europeans, but it was their own native literature,
the literature of their new America, that really excited
them. As the critic Mark Shechner writes:

> Bookish and impecunious boys who, two
> generations before, might have pored over

their Talmuds in the bleak synagogues of the Russian-Polish border, or who, a generation later, would have debated the economic interpretation of history or the fate of Western man in the ghettoes of Vilna or Bialystok or the cafes of East Side Manhattan, by the twenties and thirties had discovered Twain, Melville, and Hawthorne, and even, pursuing the vectors of the language back to their origin, the treasury of English literature and culture.

And their politics? In their own way, these critics were radicals long before university English departments became Marxist cells. Howe has been a socialist all his life; Rahv was a founder of the left-wing *Partisan Review;* Trilling was a liberal critic of liberalism. But they didn't consider it their job to lobby for opening up the canon; they weren't in the business of getting Jewish writers like Sholem Aleichem and Isaac Babel on the syllabus. Some books you read on your own.

Nor were they Anglophiles (even if some of them affected an English manner). What primarily appealed to them about English and American literature was that it was somehow *theirs.* To read Whitman's *Democratic Vistas* or Henry James's *The American Scene* (even if it did contain some brutal anti-Semitic passages) was to be infused with a spontaneous vitality, a sense of belonging to the New World in which their parents had arrived. No one has written more eloquently about the tremendous impact of this literature than Alfred Kazin. "The past, the past was great," he exulted in *A Walker in the City.* "I read as if books would fill my every gap, legitimize my strange quest for the American past, remedy my every flaw, let me in at last into the great world that was anything just out of Brownsville." To know, to possess and claim that past as one's own, was to become American.

Jews haven't been the only ones eager to celebrate what they regarded as *their* literature. As other minorities made their way up and seized the opportunities for higher education that became available to them, they responded in the same way. As a boy, Henry Louis Gates copied out passages from Charles Dickens and Jane Austen, passages that named what he "deeply felt but could not say." The black writer Maya Angelou, called upon as a child to recite a poem before her church congregation in Stamps, Arkansas, chose Portia's speech from *The Merchant of Venice.* "Nobody else understands it," she recalled, "but I *know* that William Shakespeare was a black woman. That is the role of art in life." We identify with the great characters in fiction because we recognize our own experience of the world in theirs—not because of the color of their skin.

If you're a black woman these days, you're more likely to read a book that was written by one: a Toni Morrison novel; a slave diary resurrected from some newly exhumed Civil War archive; a memoir by Maya Angelou. In the new curricular scheme of things, the books that used to be considered classics aren't as universal as we thought they were. The canon of English and American literature turns out to be a conspiracy of the dominant class. In *Sensational Designs*, Jane Tompkins quotes a famous passage in F. O. Matthiessen's *American Renaissance* in which he singles out for praise the half-decade 1850–55, which produced (among other books) Emerson's *Representative Men*, Hawthorne's *The Scarlet Letter*, Melville's *Moby-Dick*, and Whitman's *Leaves of Grass*. This list, Tompkins objects, was assigned to generations of undergraduates. What's wrong with it? It's "exclusive and class-bound," it "embodies the views of a very small, socially, culturally, geographically, sexually, and racially restricted elite." There are no works by women on Matthiessen's list; no works that deal with "the issues of abolition and temperance"; no works "by males not of Anglo-Saxon origin; and, indeed, no works by writers living south of New York, north of Boston, or west of Stockbridge, Massachusetts." So much for a reading list that purports to depict the whole soul of man.

For Tompkins, the old order is a WASP enclave, the literary equivalent of the Metropolitan Club. But does it matter? "It used to be thought that ideas transcended race, gender, and class," Gertrude Himmelfarb writes wistfully on the op-ed page of the *New York Times*, "that there are such things as truth, reason, morality, and artistic excellence, which can be understood and aspired to by everyone, of whatever race, gender, or class." Great literature is literature with a universal message. Its purpose, says Walter Jackson Bate, is to instruct us in "the whole experience of life."

What do we mean by *whole?* The right is just as "exclusionist" as the left when it comes to defining it. "The real community of man," Allan Bloom asserts, "is the community of those who seek the truth, of the potential knowers, that is, in principle, of all men to the extent they desire to know." He doesn't mean "all men," of course. If he did, there wouldn't have been so many objections to his book. The culture that he values is the culture of the West. Bloom clings to the idea that Socrates, Plato, Machiavelli, Kant, and Rousseau constitute a precious legacy; they represent the culture we've inherited. And some cultures are superior to others. As Bloom's colleague Saul Bellow so memorably put it, "Who is the Tolstoy of the Zulus? The Proust of the Papuans? I'd be glad to read him."

Bloom's message is outwardly patriotic: "The United States is one of the highest and most extreme achievements of the rational quest for the good life according to nature." But a close reading of his book makes it clear that Bloom isn't all that interested in our culture, except in the broadest sense—our culture as it derives from antiquity and the European nation-states whose achievements were built upon it, the culture whose artifacts are to be found in every museum and church in Europe. Too often, the debate over Western civilization fails to examine what anyone means by Western civilization. For Bloom and his ideological compatriots, Western civ stands for something more than Plato and Aristotle, the Great Books, the best that has been thought and said. It's a synonym for high culture, the kind of high culture *they* soaked up when they were students. "The longing for

Europe has been all but extinguished in the young," mourns Bloom. Youth worships at a different shrine now. The grand tour isn't what it was in Henry James's day, a pilgrimage to the citadels of art in Rome and Venice, Paris and London—the civilization that nourished James and George Santayana. The young still go abroad on their summer vacations, flying Virgin Atlantic with Harvard *Let's Go* guides in their backpacks; but Europe as a theater of self-improvement is obsolete.

Bloom scarcely discusses American literature in his book. The transcendentalists and their literary heirs play no part in his scheme of things. As Arthur Schlesinger, Jr., has pointed out in "The Opening of the American Mind," Bloom "spends 400 pages laying down the law about the American mind and never once mentions the two greatest and most characteristic American thinkers, Emerson and William James." Why? Schlesinger conjectures: "It is because he would have had to concede the fact that the American mind is by nature and tradition skeptical, irreverent, pluralistic, and relativistic."

Bloom would admit to the charge. Only for him, these traits are double-edged. Tolerance is no virtue; it's a license to dilute the purity of our high cultural inheritance with infusions from the crude materialistic culture that America represents. What's good about America—or what used to be good—isn't to be found on the American-literature shelf. What's good about America is our capacity for freedom, says Bloom—freedom to reason, to discriminate, to decide for oneself what is just and what is right. How do we acquire this capacity? By reading the Great Books. The *old* Great Books.

But freedom, like the whole soul of man, is hard to define. Both sides in the book wars have appropriated it. Both sides maintain that the goal of education is realizing the true self. This sounds good, but what does it mean? As I understand it, self-definition is achieved through the exercise of skepticism, challenging the status quo, learning independence of mind. To cultivate the faculty of reason is to discover one's nature. The philosopher's mandate, says Bloom, is "to know things as they are."

How to achieve that goal? Richard Rorty offers a practical solution: in order to "realize" themselves, the young must know their own history. The Revolutionary War, the Civil War, the women's suffrage movement, abolition—these events constitute, in Rorty's words, a "narrative of freedom and hope." They provide a lesson in moral conduct and values: "The point of non-vocational higher education is to help students realize that they can reshape themselves, that they can rework the self-image foisted on them by their past, the self-image that makes them competent citizens, into a new self-image, one that they themselves have helped to create."

Yes, but whose self-image? Isn't even the narrative Rorty envisions "privileged"—that is to say, the creation of a largely white, male educational establishment? What we choose to read determines how we interpret our collective past. The purportedly neglected classics that Jane Tompkins recommends— *Uncle Tom's Cabin*, Susan Warner's *The Wide, Wide*

World, the novels of Brockden Brown—aren't simply her personal best; they're propaganda weapons in a war. "The literary canon, as codified by a cultural elite, has power to influence the way the country thinks across a broad range of issues," Tompkins concludes. "The struggle now being waged in the professoriate over which writers deserve canonical status is not just a struggle over the relative merits of literary geniuses; it is a struggle among contending factions for the right to be represented in the picture America draws of itself."

Where are the women? Where are the Indians? Where are the slaves? We can't just paint them out. And even if we acknowledge them, even if we agree that our own history is the one we ought to study first, whose version are we to believe? The optimistic notion of progress inscribed in traditional approaches to American literature and history reflects a kind of literary nationalism. "America" is a myth like any other. Behind the stories our children learn in school—the Boston Tea Party, the Emancipation Proclamation, the uplifting sagas of a people determined to be free— lurk other, darker themes: racism, class struggle, the suppression of "marginalized" groups. The canon of American literature put forward by F. O. Matthiessen ignores these constituencies, Tompkins and her comrades on the literary barricades insist. Its claim to universality is spurious.

Sidney Hook, in a shrewd essay entitled "Civilization and Its Malcontents"—the last thing he wrote before his recent death at the age of 86—supplied a persuasive rebuttal to this argument. A partisan of no party, Hook was a conservative who had been a Marxist in his youth. His conservatism was tempered by a sympathy for the egalitarian impulses of the left if not for its grasp of logic. "Of course the culture of the past was created by the elite members of the past!" Hook exclaimed. "Who else could have created it at a time when literacy itself was the monopoly of the elite classes?" What no one had bothered to point out was that the very works now under attack as elitist were themselves profoundly radical. Rousseau's *Confessions*, Milton's *Areopagitica*, and Thoreau's *Walden* were among the most eloquent critiques of established authority ever produced. And even revolutionary thinkers were known to admire the classics of those cultures whose politics they deplored. Marx himself acknowledged that while Greek art and culture were the products of a class society, "they still prevail as the standard and model beyond attainment."

Hook also disposed of the notion that undergraduates should study their own racial and ethnic literature. Art is supposed to hold a mirror up to nature, not to the artist. "Does one have to be French to study or understand Napoleon, Russian to understand Lenin, Greek to read Homer or enjoy the figures of Praxiteles?" he asked.

> [We might] as well argue that men cannot be good gynecologists, that only women with children can best understand and administer family law, that only fat physicians can study obesity, and hungry ones the physiology of

starvation as to assert or imply that only people of color or women are uniquely qualified
to do justice, wherever relevant, to the
place, achievements, and oppressions of
minorities and their culture.

Hook's argument, unlike Gertrude Himmelfarb's
appeal to "truth, reason, morality, and artistic excellence," is pragmatic: the classics of our culture do
have an impact on how we see the world. The greatest
works, the works that endure to influence successive
generations, are those possessed of the broadest vision—a vision that is progressive if not revolutionary.
They challenge our self-image as a society, force us to
examine its failings as well as its strengths. And to
achieve this end, no minority credentials are required.

What *is* required is a knowledge of the American
past. Our schools are now producing a generation that
has scarcely heard of the civil rights movement, much
less the Civil War, much less the primary documents—the Constitution, the Declaration of Independence, the Bill of Rights—that make up our written
heritage. In a time when so many of the values that
govern our society have eroded, when the channels of
transmission—religion, literature, a knowledge of history—no longer function, we're faced with a new phenomenon. The French cultural critic Tzvetan Todorov
describes it as "deculturation." We are producing a
generation that has no stake in our society; its ways
and customs mean nothing to them. And the consequences of this radical alienation are evident in the
conditions of near anarchy that prevail in our cities.

The fabric of America's social order is wearing thin. Deculturation prefigures disintegration.

What is culture? In a talk given before the American Council of Learned Societies in 1987, Roger Shattuck offered three definitions:

> 1. Official rituals and ceremonies and celebrations; monuments like the Statue of Liberty; the flag; the national anthem; the pledge of allegiance.
> 2. A loose, shared store of stories (legendary and historic); folklore (including proverbs); ideas and concepts; historical and presumed facts.
> 3. A collection of concrete, lasting works (images, buildings, music, writings in poetry and prose) considered significant or great or beautiful.

Shattuck, best-known as the author of an erudite and entertaining book about Paris in the twenties called *The Banquet Years,* is identified with neither the right nor the left. His mission is to make sure that students learn, that the culture to which he's devoted his life remains intact. The values his definition of culture presupposes—"human continuity, greatness, and recognition of them in masterworks"—are basic to the humanities, key elements of any effort to appreciate a work of art. They don't answer the objections of New Canonists determined to renovate the curriculum; they simply posit that there *is* a core tradition in the humanities. That core is our cultural legacy. "It is perfectly natural that the tradition one first acquires be that of the country in which one lives," writes Tzvetan Todorov—"perfectly natural, therefore, that Americans should master the American tradition."

This is E. D. Hirsch's point. What should Americans know? Their own heritage. Why? Because the culture in which they live reflects that heritage. "To teach the ways of one's own community has always been and still remains the essence of the education of our children, who enter neither a narrow tribal culture nor a transcendent world culture but a national literate culture." In support of this contention, Hirsch quotes from the preface to a series of schoolbooks popular at the turn of the century, *Everyday Classics:*

> In an age when the need of socializing and unifying our people is keenly felt, the value of a common stock of knowledge, a common set of ideals, is obvious. A people is best unified by being taught in childhood the best things in its intellectual and moral heritage. Our own heritage is, like our ancestry, composite. Hebrew, Greek, Roman, English, French, and Teutonic elements are blended in our cultural past. . . . An introduction to the best of this is one of our ways of making good citizens.

Why do we study English and American literature? Not to prove its superiority, not to impose upon minorities a literature that's alien to their experience.

We study it, Hirsch explains, "for purely functional reasons," because our literature is the medium through which our language—the essence of our culture—is transmitted and preserved. And to be schooled in that culture, to know one's way around it, is to define our collective identity—as Hirsch puts it, "to decide what 'American' means on the other side of the hyphen in Italo-American or Asian-American."

This is no easy matter. One of the main weaknesses of the American federation of states is that it's such an amalgam of diverse interests and identities. The rhetoric of our primary documents affirms a vision of America to which most of us assent; but those documents were framed by a dissenting elite for a nation that consisted of a few thousand souls. How are we to address the vastly different constituency that has emerged since the white, male Founding Fathers sat down with their quill pens to compose their decrees? A lot of troubling developments have interfered with their original vision, notably the absorption of a populace more various and—in the case of blacks and Hispanics—more resistant to assimilation than they could ever have imagined. How should we teach this populace American history and literature? Maybe we should let our students learn these subjects the way earlier generations did—aspiring to become a part of the America they read about. They can decide for themselves where they stand.

In his essay "The Opening of the American Mind," Arthur Schlesinger, Jr., made a persuasive case for this solution. "For better or for worse," he wrote, "we inherit an American experience, as America inherits a Western experience; and solid learning must begin with our own origins and tradition." The values embodied in the works we teach and in our common rituals are the only ones we have. "History has given them to us," Schlesinger concludes. "They are anchored in our national experience, in our great national documents, in our national heroes, in our folkways, tradition, standards. They work for us; and, for that reason, we live and die by them."

Seven

We Are What We Read

"No one believes in greatness," said Walter Jackson Bate one afternoon when we were talking in his office at Harvard. "That's gone."

I gazed around the professor's comfortable room on the second floor of Warren House. The musty, worn volumes on their varnished shelves exuded a civilized air. Twenty years out of college, I wasn't *that* old; it was premature for me to cluck about the crisis in our universities like some patrician, crusty grad, class of '26, in the letters column of the college alumni magazine. But it was hard not to sympathize with Bate's elegiac note. Something had ended. There was no going back.

Was it my own undergraduate days I was nostalgic for, or had the world really changed? A few weeks later, browsing among my books, I stumbled upon this passage from an essay, "Our Age Among the Ages," by John Crowe Ransom:

> Now, I am in the education business, and I can report my observations on that. It is as if a sudden invasion of barbarians had overrun the educational institution. . . . We should not fear them; they are not foreigners, nor our enemies. But in the last resort education is a democratic process, in which the courses are subject to the election of the applicants, and a course even when it has been elected can never rise above the intellectual passion of its pupils, or their comparative indifference. So, with the new generation of students, Milton declines in the curriculum; even Shakespeare has lost heavily; Homer and Virgil are practically gone. The literary interest of the students today is 90 percent in the literature of their own age; more often than not it is found in books which do not find entry into the curriculum, and are beneath the standard which your humble servants, the teachers of literature, are trying to maintain. Chaucer and Spenser and Milton, with their respective contemporaries, will

have their existence henceforth in the library, and of course in the love and intimate acquaintance of a certain academic community, and there they will stay except for possible periods when there is a revival of the literature of our own antiquity. Our literary culture for a long time is going to exist in a sprawling fashion, with minority pockets of old-style culture, and some sort of majority culture of a new and indeterminate style. It is a free society, and I should expect that the rights of minorities will be as secure as the rights of individuals.

That was written in 1958.

Once in a while, leafing through the current Harvard catalogue as I pursue my curricular research, I come across a course description that stirs me: "The English Bible," for instance, "an introduction to the Hebrew Bible and New Testament with special attention to narrative modes, figures of the human and divine, ethical problems, and sacred mysteries." Or: "The Nineteenth-Century English Novel," which offers "readings in several of the century's major novelists, including Austen, Scott, the Brontës, Dickens, Thackeray, Eliot, Hardy." Even these apparently straightforward offerings haven't escaped a brush with the *zeitgeist*. The novels aren't simply to be read; they're to be read with an "emphasis on the generic, historical, ideological, and theoretical implications of the texts." Still, books are books. (Or should I say, texts are texts.) Just reading over the authors' names is enough to awaken powerful memories.

It was in a state of intense anticipation that I made my way through this very same catalogue each year when it came in the mail toward the end of the summer, a few weeks before the beginning of the fall semester. Then, as now, the catalogue was as thick as a Russian novel, and crammed with exotic offerings in Sanskrit, Serbo-Croatian, Medieval Greek. But it was the offerings in English and American literature that compelled my attention. The Reformation, Cromwell, English political philosophy—reading Trevelyan's *History of England* in the cavernous main reading room of Widener Library late at night, the radiators hissing and clanking, the air stale with cigarette smoke (it really *was* a long time ago), I was mesmerized by the power of ideas.

What was this power? How to describe it? Surely I had only the feeblest grasp of the ideas themselves. What did Locke actually mean by natural rights? What was Hobbes's notion of the state? What I remember best is the books themselves, the physical objects, austere pocket-sized volumes in navy blue—*The Rights of Man, On Liberty, Areopagitica*—that I still have on my shelves. It was the sheer sensation of learning that excited me, of beginning to master chronology. The blur of names and dates that I found so daunting in September would become, by winter reading period, a coherent narrative. There was *Beowulf, Sir Gawain and the Green Knight*, Chaucer, Spenser, the Elizabethan poets and playwrights, the seventeenth-century metaphysicals, the neoclassical poets, the Romantics, the Victorians, the Georgians, and finally, the modern poets, the poets I'd read in high school: Eliot and Yeats and Auden. A vivid, busy procession that stretched over a thousand years, from England's origins to the present. The moment in which I lived.

How much do I retain now of what I read? Not a great deal. I have faint memories of Emerson's essays, a few lines of Whitman—"I am the man, I suffered, I was there"—a dim awareness of the plot of *Billy Budd*. (The sailor hangs.) Most of it has vanished. What actually happens in *The Scarlet Letter*? Who was the Faerie Queene?

Nor do I often go back to these books. Sometimes, though, as I hurry past the shelves where they sit in orderly rows—the volumes of Virginia Woolf's *Diary*, the Faber editions of T. S. Eliot's prose, the Macmillan edition of Yeats—I find myself thinking back to those winter nights in Widener when I read for no worldly purpose, no hope of gain. When the world expected nothing of me, and my whole purpose in life was to work my way through *The Norton Anthology of English Literature*. At midnight, when the library closed, I would walk out into Harvard Yard, down the icy marble steps, inhaling the crisp New England air, hauling my books in an olive-green canvas book bag back to my dorm, ready to spend the next three hours boning up on the Enclosure Act.

The chronologies, footnotes, and appendices—all this apparatus of learning—gave scholarly weight to the books I read. They imposed a gloss of erudition. But I always read for the story. What happened next?

Racing through Trevelyan's monumental *History of England,* I was enthralled by his dramatic evocation of long ago, "the era of Celt, Saxon, and Dane." This was no dry treatise. A master of English prose, Trevelyan conjured up England from its earliest beginnings, a primitive, ancient world of "giant figures," "warriors at strife," the air reverberant with "the cry of seamen beaching their ships." I've forgotten what domesday was, and whether Henry II came before Richard I. What I remember was realizing how old our civilization is, what a miracle that so much of its history is still intact.

What was that line of Eliot's? *"History is now and England."* But it was also America—America before my time. I read *The Education of Henry Adams,* the three-volume autobiography of Henry James, Malcolm Cowley's *Exile's Return,* the journalism of Edmund Wilson. They weren't the kind of books that made for a classical education, but they were highly informative. They gave me a sense of the author's life, and told a story that taught by example. What did they teach? In the largest sense, I suppose, that certain experiences are universal—that "the very condition of being human," in Roger Shattuck's words, "is not given but learned." And what better way to understand that condition than to read about others like ourselves—not in the particulars of class or ethnic identity, but in the recognition that we share with them a common heritage?

One of the most striking features of the reading lists I've come across in various essays and memoirs by American writers is how eclectic they are. There's always been a core of sorts. "When I was an under-graduate in Chicago, we were told not to bother with humanist scholars but to study the Great Books them-selves," Saul Bellow recalls. "Bright undergraduates from the slums, the suburbs, or the sticks agreed that the *Phaedrus* or *Hamlet* was exactly what they should be reading." It was a core defined by personal predi-lections, not by politics. Ralph Ellison, growing up in Macon County, Georgia, read Marx, Freud, T. S. Eliot, Gertrude Stein, and Hemingway. Richard Ro-driguez, the son of Mexican immigrants, grew up speaking Spanish; the product of a "socially disadvan-taged" milieu, he worked his way through Stanford and Columbia and managed to become a writer. His memoir, *Hunger of Memory,* is one of the few books to describe the American education of a Third World immigrant. What did Rodriguez read as a boy grap-pling with English? Hawthorne's *The Scarlet Letter,* Kipling, *The Babe Ruth Story, Moby-Dick, Gone With the Wind, The Good Earth,* and "the entire first vol-ume of the *Encyclopaedia Britannica*—A through AN-STEY." What mattered wasn't what one read; it was that one read at all.

Apart from a few hard-liners, no one's demand-ing that schools institute a uniform curriculum. The basic syllabus can be altered and survive. "The canon is neither immutable nor totally malleable," observes Tzvetan Todorov. Every age has its own sacred texts. In the eighteenth century, the classics were the means by which "the West's concern for the connection of the here and now to the abiding was preserved, trans-mitted, and carried on," explains Bruce Kuklick, Mellon Professor of the Humanities at the University of Pennsylvania. In the nineteenth century, philosophy and religion figured largely in the syllabus; the Bible was required reading. The celebrated Harvard Humanist Irving Babbitt expected concentrators in English literature to know the primary medieval authors: Dante, Petrarch, Boccaccio. When I attended Oxford in the early 1970s, you couldn't graduate in English without having mastered Sweet's *Anglo-Saxon Grammar*. No living writer was taught; the syllabus ended with Yeats. Auden, sitting alone in the St. Aldate's Coffee House, didn't qualify.

Yet none of this was writ in stone. "I do not see what *literary* culture our undergraduates can possibly derive from any English writings anterior to Chaucer's," objected Professor James Morgan Hart, noting that *Beowulf* was "as foreign to our way of thinking as if it had been expressed in a foreign tongue." He wrote that in *PMLA* in 1884. As for courses in contemporary literature, they're nothing new. A hundred years ago, William Lyon Phelps of Yale proposed a course on modern novels, insisting that "there was no reason why the literature of 1895 could not be made as suitable a subject for college study as the literature of 1295."

Literary canons are made very much the way literature is made: by a process of transformation. To cite T.S. Eliot's famous account of canon shifts in "Tradition and the Individual Talent":

What happens when a new work of art is created is something that happens simulta-

neously to all the works of art which pre-
ceded it. The existing monuments form an
ideal order among themselves, which is
modified by the new (the really new) work of
art among them. The existing order is com-
plete before the new work arrives; for order
to persist after the supervention of novelty,
the *whole* existing order must be, if ever so
slightly, altered; and so the relations, pro-
portions, values of each work of art toward
the whole are readjusted; and this is con-
formity between the old and the new.

Whenever a previously neglected author is discovered
or restored to favor or promoted to classic status by
the academic benediction of a college reading list, that
author's inclusion changes—or ought to change—our
conception of the whole syllabus. By what criteria was
this author chosen? What does his—or her!—inclusion say about the canon and how the works that compose it are chosen, how the past reverberates in the
present?

You don't have to be a conservative to make the
conservative case. Edward Said, a professor of comparative literature at Columbia, teaches such apparently "marginal" works as Ghassan Kanafani's *Men
in the Sun,* about the tragic fate of three Palestinian
refugees, and *Season of Migration to the North,* a
novel by Tayib Salih about a young Sudanese who
returns from London to his ancestral home on the
Nile. Meritorious in their own right, such works open
up to us, says Said, "a whole world of other literatures

and formal articulations." They bring us to "an appreciation not of some tiny, defensively constituted corner of the world, but of the large many-windowed house of human culture as a whole." In the end, exposure to these other literatures and cultures makes us more tolerant. "To 'decenter' our viewpoint, to break free from egocentric and ethnocentric illusions, we must learn to become detached from ourselves," maintains Tzvetan Todorov. "There is only one way to achieve this; by confronting our norms with those of other people, by discovering that they, too, are legitimate."

To hope for a consensus on the curriculum is futile; diversity is the essence of a democratic society. But diversity has its limits. "Even a randomly picked group of intelligent and educated people will agree on a handful of books that everyone should read at some point, in some form," Roger Shattuck asserts. What books? It wouldn't be hard to come up with a provisional list: the standard works of Aristotle and Plato, St. Augustine, Machiavelli, Montaigne, Rousseau, Shakespeare, Milton, Dante; the English political philosophers who inspired those documents that make up the written heritage of our own government; selections from the literature of one European language, read in that language; the King James Bible; and a sample of American literature—as it was before the New Americanists got to it. The Library of America, a series of volumes devoted to reprinting the classics of American literature, runs to some sixty volumes so far, in handsome editions unburdened by scholarly apparatus, from the works of Abraham Lincoln to Harriet

Beecher Stowe, Ralph Waldo Emerson to Eugene O'Neill, Willa Cather to Henry James. Plans are now afoot to reprint paperback editions of this series: why not adopt them in our schools?

Think of the books we read in high school (my informal poll has turned up a virtually uniform list): *Hamlet; J. B.*, a play by Archibald MacLeish; F. Scott Fitzgerald's *The Great Gatsby;* James Joyce's *Dubliners;* George Eliot's *Silas Marner;* John Steinbeck's *Of Mice and Men;* Hemingway's *The Old Man and the Sea.* What do these books have in common? Why are they assigned by high school teachers year after year? They're easy to read, for one thing; they're written with a simplicity and economy that makes them (or made them) readily comprehensible to the average sixteen-year-old; they're pitched at the right level. More important, they seem familiar. MacLeish's play is loosely based on the Book of Job; *Hamlet* is perhaps Shakespeare's most accessible play, the great speeches so often quoted they've become part of our everyday language; Hemingway is a showcase of the American vernacular; *Dubliners* has the classic simplicity of a hymn. Is it any wonder that students identify with these books? They're the lore of our culture.

This isn't to say that we should ignore minority literature, Third World literature, the literature of peoples around the globe. But without a common culture, a culture that possesses certain shared assumptions, there will soon be no America to imagine, no common myth around which to organize our aspirations. The study of American literature invests us in our own society by enabling us to recognize ourselves in it—to find there a general representation of our experience.

What does one learn from these works? That English literature is the primary source of the language that we speak, a living organism, evolved through centuries of use, and thus a repository of our culture's most enduring traditions, the written record of its past. In a practical sense, one also learns the kind of elemental mastery that used to be taken for granted—how to read and write one's own language. (It's not surprising that corporations have begun to recruit humanities majors: they're the only ones who are still literate.)

Sidney Hook, summing up his position on the curricular debate in a 1989 article in the *American Scholar*, listed six things that students "need to know, whether they know it or not." Every student needs to learn how to communicate clearly and effectively, to express himself in a literate way; to have a rudimentary grasp of the natural world, of evolution and genetics; to comprehend the historical, economic, and social forces that have shaped our collective destiny; to know something about religion and morality; to acquire the capacity to reason; and to be "inducted into the cultural legacies of his civilization, its art, literature, and music."

Utopian proposals, perhaps, inspired by a time when Hook was training the best immigrant minds of his generation at New York University; a time before urban high schools were overwhelmed by crime and drugs; before a population arose that was excluded from any hope of a better life. In a way it seems futile to discuss the curriculum, to debate which books students ought to read, when—especially in inner-city schools—many of them can't read at all. "If we do not provide adequate knowledge to fill those hungry minds and empty schoolroom hours, something else will," warns Roger Shattuck. "That something else may well be deadening and corrupting—estrangement, anomie, idle vandalism, drugs, crime, suicide. These things cannot be said too often."

But saving our schools isn't just a matter of improving test scores or teaching children to read. There has to be some agreement about what it is we wish them to know. Yale's black studies program is in disarray: several members of the department have defected, and those who remain lack a sense of purpose or direction. Why is this? In part because they can't agree on what to study. There are courses of instruction in the Hausa, Yoruba, and Zulu languages; Swahili literature; and "Psychological Perspectives on African-American Experiences in the United States." The field is wide—inchoate, the faculty complains. Furthermore, it tends to attract minority students, fostering a kind of unintentional segregation. Only now, more than two decades after the founding of African-American studies, are the consequences of this trend toward ethnic specialization becoming clear. In jettisoning the idea of a canon of Great Books, we've undermined what used to be our primary educational goal: the transmission of a body of works arrived at through decades, even centuries of debate. "We're still at the point of resurrecting texts," says Henry Louis Gates, who is busy establishing a canon of his own with the forthcoming *Norton Anthology of African-American Literature*. "We have to produce the tradition, *then* we have to analyze it." That's all well and good; but why not read the tradition that's there?

It's pointless to mourn the days when everyone read the classics. Things have gone too far. The curricular revolution is entrenched; the students are militant; the class of educated citizens that once prided itself on a knowledge of European culture has dwindled to virtually nothing. Cynthia Ozick describes the situation with elegiac fervor: "High art is dead. The passion for inheritance is dead. Tradition is equated with obscurantism. The wall that divided serious high culture from the popular arts is breached; anything can count as 'text.'"

In the generation to come, there won't even be an audience for this art. The "Anglo-Saxon cultural values" decried in the Sobol report are a thing of the past. The bow-tied English professors who promoted them have all gone into the dark. As even David Rieff, a self-styled radical, says with some acerbity, "Whatever the future is, it isn't white."

Educating the next generation will be a difficult task. What's essential is to preserve and affirm the idea of basic literacy, of learning grounded in a core of knowledge. Bloom derides Mortimer Adler, one of the founders of the Great Books program at the University of Chicago, as an equal-opportunity intellectual, and there *is* an element of showmanship in Adler's hawking of high culture; but when he shows up at Goldblatt Elementary School on the city's destitute West Side to conduct a seminar on *Hamlet* with children from the housing projects, he's working on behalf of what has always been a part of the American dream: culture as a path to self-improvement. My grandmother had on the shelf in her Rogers Park living room blue Pelican paperbacks of Kant and Kierkegaard. They were coming apart at the spine. I have no idea what she made of them, but I'm sure something got through, if only the idea that there *were* ideas. To be thoroughly modern, to be an American, was to know about these books—to be educated. The mere possession of them was a sign that she'd arrived.

Why did Allan Bloom and E. D. Hirsch become the intellectual superstars of the late 1980s? The tremendous commercial success of their books reflected this immigrant hunger to learn. But they also had a message. They had discovered a potential threat to our society and they gave warning. America is foundering because Americans no longer get a proper education. In their attempts to redress injustice, the radicals of the 1960s unwittingly helped to perpetuate it; the assault on the curriculum has undermined the foundation of learning on which our society rests. The problem can be simply put: What we don't know will hurt us. And it has.

In style, these two prophets of cultural doom could hardly be more unalike. Hirsch is the practical one: his book is a primer on how to make our educational system work. Bloom is more theoretical: his book appeals to the perennial student in us—that yearning, after years out in the busy world, to restore for a brief moment the innocence of our undergraduate days, the long nights in the library spent struggling through *The Social Contract*. In the end, *The Closing of the American Mind* is about the joys of education:

how to live in the world without losing one's soul.

Hirsch is a booster. He wants America to be great again, and to assert its greatness as a culture. Bloom likes the opportunities America affords even as he holds its culture in contempt. But their basic message is the same. "Just as in politics the responsibility for the fate of freedom in the world has devolved upon our regime, so the fate of philosophy in the world has devolved upon our universities, and the two are related as they have never been before," writes Bloom on the last page of his book. "The gravity of our given task is great, and it is very much in doubt how the future will judge our stewardship." What we read, he's saying—*if* we read—will determine America's fate.

This can all seem very abstract, despite the urgency with which our two prophets deliver the bad news. What do the Great Books have to do with the fragile edifice of culture? Doesn't it always need shoring up against the forces of barbarism? To my mind, the connection isn't fanciful. The new curriculum is an effort to validate the claims of the individual. But what about the claims of society? Who will argue on its behalf? Only a nation schooled in its own past can grasp the negotiation between personal freedom and collective self-interest that is the essence of our American democracy. Those ideas are learned in books. The Great Books. The best that is known and thought in the world. The canon.

Until a few years ago, this was our educational mandate. If it goes, a tradition that we cherished will go with it.

Notes on Sources

FOREWORD

The quotation from Matthew Arnold on page 12 is from "The Function of Criticism at the Present Time," *The Portable Matthew Arnold*, ed. Lionel Trilling (New York, 1949), p. 265.

The metaphor of "Balkanization" on page 12 occurs in Robert Hughes's essay, "The Fraying of America," *Time* (February 3, 1992), p. 47.

The reference to Arthur M. Schlesinger, Jr., on page 13 is to his book *The Disuniting of America: Reflections on a Multicultural Society* (New York, 1992).

Mary Louise Pratt's quotation on page 13 is from "Humanities for the Future: Reflections on the Western Culture Debate at Stanford," *The Politics of Liberal Education*, ed. Darryl J. Gless and Barbara Herrnstein Smith (Durham, N.C., 1992), p. 15.

Dinesh d'Souza's quotation on page 14 is from his book *Illiberal Education: The Politics of Race and Sex on Campus* (New York, 1991), p. 13.

Hilton Kramer's quotation on page 15 is from his article "The Academic Left Strikes Back," *New Criterion* (November 1991).

Henry Louis Gates, Jr.'s quotation on page 14 is from his article "The Master's Pieces: On Canon Formation and the African American Tradition," *New York Times Book Review* (February 26, 1989).

Richard Rorty's essay, as quoted on pages 15–16 can be found in *The Politics of Liberal Education*, ed. Gless and Smith.

David Bromwich's remarks on page 18 appear in his article "Canon Bashing," *Dissent* (Fall 1988), p. 479.

Jerome Christensen's quotations on page 18 are from his article "From Rhetoric to Corporate Populism: A Romantic Critique of the Academy in an Age of High Gossip," *Critical Inquiry* (Spring 1990).

John Searle's article, mentioned on page 18, appeared in *New York Review of Books* (December 6, 1990); Irving Howe's article appeared in *The New Republic* (February 18, 1991); and Louis Menand's article appeared in *Harper's* (December 1991).

Paul Berman's quotation on page 18 is from his book *Debating P.C.: The Controversy over Political Correctness on College Campuses* (New York, 1992), p. 26.

Stanley Fish's essay, referred to on page 19, is reprinted in *The Politics of Liberal Education*, ed. Gless and Smith.

The quotation from Cardinal John Henry Newman on page 20 is from his book *The Idea of a University* (New York, 1947), p. 98.

ONE: THE WARNING

Arthur Schlesinger, Jr.'s quotation on page 27 is from his article "The Opening of the American Mind," *New York Times Book Review*, July 23, 1989.

David Rieff's quotation on page 27 appears in his article "The Colonel and the Professor," *London Times Literary Supplement*, September 4, 1987.

Allan Bloom's quotations on pages 27–32 are from his book *The Closing of the American Mind* (New York, 1987), pp. 75, 348.

Walter Jackson Bate's quotation on page 29 is from his article "The Crisis in English Studies," *Harvard Magazine* (Sept–Oct 1982).

Lynne V. Cheney's quotations on pages 33–34 are from her pamphlet "Humanities in America: A Report to the President, the Congress, and the American People" (Washington, D.C., The National Endowment for the Arts, September 1988).

William Bennett's quotations on page 34 can be found in his article "Why the West?" *National Review*, May 27, 1988.

Francis Fukuyama's quotations on page 36 are from his article "The End of History," *National Interest*, no. 16 (Summer 1989).

TWO: THE BIG BOYS

Gerald Graff's remark on page 40 is quoted in my article, "The Battle of the Books," *New York Times Magazine*, June 5, 1988.

Lionel Trilling's quotation on page 42 is from his article "The Uncertain Future of the Humanistic Educational Ideal," *American Scholar* (Winter 1974–75), p. 58.

The quotation on page 44 is from Daniel Bell and Irving Kristol, *Confrontation: The Student Rebellion and the University* (New York, 1969), p. 47.

George Kennan's quotation on page 44 is from "Rebels without a Program," *New York Times Magazine*, January 21, 1968, p. 22.

Allan Bloom's quotation on page 45 is from his book *The Closing of the American Mind*, p. 320.

Paul de Man's quotations on pages 45–46 are from "Hypogram and Inscription," in his book *The Resistance to Theory* (Minneapolis, 1986), pp. 27–53.

The article cited on page 48, "U.S. Literature: Canon Under Siege," appeared in *New York Times*, January 6, 1988.

THREE: THE NEW CANONISTS

Jane Tompkins's quotation on page 55 is from her book *Sensational Designs: The Cultural Work of American Fiction 1790–1860* (New York, 1985), p. 35.

Clement Greenberg's quotation on page 58 is from "Under Forty," *Contemporary Jewish Record* (February 1944), p. 33.

Diana Trilling's quotation on pages 58–59 is from her memoir "Lionel Trilling: A Jew at Columbia," in Lionel Trilling, *Speaking of Literature and Society* (New York, 1980), p. 422.

Frank Lentricchia's quotation on page 59 is from his book *Criticism and Social Change* (Chicago, 1983).

Egon Mayer's quotation on page 60 is from Joseph Berger, "Sociology's Long Decade in the Wilderness," *New York Times*, May 28, 1989, Week in Review, p. 6.

The New Historian's remark on page 61 is quoted in "History with the Politics Left Out," from Gertrude Himmelfarb, *The New History and the Old: Critical Essays and Reappraisals* (Cambridge, 1987), p. 13.

Barbara Herrnstein Smith's quotation on page 65 is from her book *Contingencies of Value* (Cambridge, Mass. 1988), p. 27.

D.A. Miller's quotation on page 66 is from his book *The Novel and the Police*, (Berkeley, 1988), p. 137.

FOUR: THE DECLINE OF LITERARY CRITICISM

R.W.B. Lewis's quotation on page 68 is from remarks delivered in 1988 at the Annual Meeting of the American Studies Association in New York.

Hilton Kramer's quotation on pages 70–71 is from his article "The Prospect Before Us," in *New Criterion*, September, 1990.

Frederick Crews's quotation on page 72 is from his article "Whose American Renaissance?" in *New York Review of Books*, October 27, 1988.

Lawrence Lipking's quotation on page 74 is from his article "Competitive Reading," in *New Republic*, October 2, 1989.

Jonathan Freedman's quotation on pages 74–75 is from his article "Auto-canonization: Tropes of Self-Legitimation in 'Popular Culture,'" *Yale Journal of Criticism;* excerpted in *Harper's* (January 1989), p. 32.

Barbara Johnson's quotation on page 75 is from her book *The Critical Difference: Essays in the Contemporary Rhetoric of Reading* (Baltimore, 1985), p. 103.

Lionel Trilling's quotation on page 76 is from his article "The Uncertain Future of the Humanistic Educational Ideal," *American Scholar* (Winter 1974–75).

Edmund Wilson's article, cited on page 77, "The Fruits of the MLA," appears in his collection, *The Devils and Canon Barham* (New York, 1973).

Roger Kimball's account of the 1990 MLA convention referred to on page 78 originally appeared in *New Criterion* (February 1991) and is reprinted in Paul Berman's anthology *Debating P.C.*

The quotations on pages 81, 82, and 83 are from "Speaking for the Humanities," *American Council of Learned Societies: Occasional Paper No. 7*, ed. George Levine (Washington, D.C.).

George Levine's quotation on page 83 is from his article "Graff Revisited," *Raritan*, Vol. 8, no. 4 (Spring, 1989).

William Barrett's quotation on page 84 is from his book *The Truants: Adventures Among the Intellectuals* (New York, 1982), p. 87.

Alfred Kazin's quotation on page 84 is from his article "The New Republic: A Personal View," *New Republic*, November 6, 1989.

Robert Nisbet's quotations on page 85 are from his book *The Degradation of the Academic Dogma: The University in America 1945–1970* (New York, 1971), p. 36.

F.R. Leavis's quotation on page 86 is borrowed from T.S. Eliot's *The Function of Criticism*, and is quoted on p. v of his preface to *The Common Pursuit* (New York, 1984).

Louis Menand's quotation on page 86 is from his article, "What is the University For? A Professor's View," *Harper's*.

Chester Finn's quotation on page 87 is from *We Must Take Charge: Our Schools and Our Future* (New York, 1991), p. 213.

Gertrude Himmelfarb's quotations on page 88 are from her essay "History With the Politics Left Out," in *The New History and the Old*, p. 23.

My account of the Sobol report mentioned on page 88 is based on articles in the *New York Times* on June 21, 22, and July 16, 1991; Nathan Glazer, "In Defense of Multiculturalism," *New Republic* (September 2, 1991); and Heather MacDonald, "The Sobol Report: Multiculturalism Triumphant," *New Criterion* (January 1992).

FIVE: CULTURAL ILLITERACY

E.D. Hirsch's quotations on pages 91, 92, and 93 are from his book *Cultural Literacy: What Every American Needs to Know* (Boston, 1987), pp. 28, 145.

Barbara Herrnstein Smith's article mentioned on page 94 appears in the collection *The Politics of Liberal Education*, ed. Gless and Smith.

E.D. Hirsch's quotation on page 96 is from his article "The Primal Scene of Education," *New York Review of Books*, March 2, 1989.

Jerry Doolittle's anecdotes mentioned on page 96 are recounted in Richard Marius, "Reflections on the Freshman English Course" in *Teaching Literature: What Is Needed Now*, ed. James Engell and David Perkins (Cambridge, 1989), p. 179; Richard Marius's own quotation is on p. 178.

The quotation from Katha Pollitt's essay "Why Do We Read?" on page 97 originally appeared in the *Nation*, (September 23, 1991), p. 328 and has been reprinted in Paul Berman's anthology *Debating P.C.*

The quotation from *The Crimson* on page 99 appears in Caleb Nelson, "Harvard's Hollow 'Core,' " *Atlantic* (September 1990), p. 80.

Richard Rorty's quotation on page 100 is from his essay "Two Cheers for the Cultural Left," in *The Politics of Liberal Education*, ed. Gless and Smith, p. 236.

SIX: THE END OF TRADITION

Cyril Connolly's quotation on page 103 is from his book *Enemies of Promise* (London, 1973), p. 167.

David Bromwich's quotation on pages 105–106 is from his article "The Future of Tradition: Notes on the Crisis in the Humanities," *Dissent* (Fall 1989).

The quotation from Ralph Waldo Emerson on page 106 appears in Irving Howe's essay, "The Treason of the Critics," *New Republic*, June 12, 1989.

Mark Shechner's quotation on page 108 is from his essay "Jewish Writers," in *The Harvard Guide to Contemporary American Writing*, ed. Daniel Hoffman (Cambridge, Mass., 1979), p. 194.

Saul Bellow's quotation on page 107 is from "Starting Out in Chicago," *American* Scholar (Winter 1974–75), p. 73.

Alfred Kazin's quotation on page 109 is from his book *A Walker in the City* (New York, 1951), p. 170.

Henry Louis Gates's quotation on page 109 is from his essay "The Master's Pieces: On Canon Formation and the African-American Tradition," in *The Politics of Liberal Education*, ed. Gless and Smith, p. 95.

Jane Tompkins's quotation on page 110 is from her book *Sensational Designs*, pp. 199–200.

Gertrude Himmelfarb's quotation on page 110 is from her essay "Stanford and Duke Undercut Classical Values," *New York Times*, Op Ed page, May 5, 1988.

Allan Bloom's quotations on pages 111 and 112 are from his book *The Closing of the American Mind*, pp. 34, 315.

Saul Bellow's remark on page 111 is from my article, "Allan Bloom: Chicago's Grumpy Guru," *New York Times Magazine* January 3, 1988.

Arthur Schlesinger, Jr.s' quotations on page 112 are from his essay "The Opening of the American Mind," *New York Times Book Review*, July 23, 1989.

Jane Tompkins's quotations on page 116 are from her book *Sensational Designs*, p. 201.

Sidney Hook's quotations on pages 115 and 116 are from his essay "Civilization and its Malcontents," *National Review*, October 13, 1989.

Tzvetan Todorov's quotation on page 116 is from his essay "How to Fill Those Empty Heads: A Cure for the Humanities Crisis," *New Republic*, July 3, 1989.

Roger Shattuck's quotations on page 117 are from "Perplexing Dreams: Is There a Core Tradition in the Humanities?" *American Council of Learned Societies: Occasional Paper No. 2* (Washington, D.C.).

E.D. Hirsch's quotations on page 118 are from his book *Cultural Literacy*, p. 18.

SEVEN: WE ARE WHAT WE READ

Walter Jackson Bate's remark on page 121 appears in my article, "The Battle of the Books."

John Crowe Ransom's quotation on page 122 is from a 1958 lecture, "Our Age Among the Ages," cited in Stanley Edgar Hyman, *The Promised End: Essays and Reviews 1942–1962* (Cleveland, 1963), p. 378.

Richard Rodriguez's quotation on page 127 is from his book *Hunger of Memory* (Boston, 1981), p. 61.

Bruce Kuklick's quotation on page 127 is from his essay "The Emergence of the Humanities," in *The Politics of Liberal Education*, ed. Gless and Smith, p. 209.

The quotation from James Morgan Hart on page 128 appears in *The Origins of Literary Studies in America: A Documentary Anthology,* ed. Gerald Graff and Michael Warner (New York, 1989), p. 36.

William Lyon Phelps's quotation on page 128 is from the excerpt "Autobiography with Letters" in *The Origins of Literary Studies in America,* ed. Graff and Warner, p. 165.

The quotation from T.S. Eliot on pages 128 and 129 appears in "Tradition and the Individual Talent," *Selected Prose of T.S. Eliot* (New York, 1975), p. 38.

Edward Said's quotation on page 130 is from his essay "The Politics of Knowledge," *Raritan* (Summer 1991).

Tzvetan Todorov's quotation on page 130 is from his essay "How to Fill Those Empty Heads?" in *New Republic.*

Sidney Hook's quotation on page 132 is from his article "The Closing of the American Mind: An Intellectual Best-Seller Revisited," *American Scholar* (Winter 1989).

Cynthia Ozick's quotation on page 134 is from her essay "A Critic at Large: T.S. Eliot at 101," *New Yorker* (November 20, 1989).

David Reiff's quotation on page 134 is from his column in *Salmagundi* (Winter 1989).

Allan Bloom's quotation on page 136 is from his book *The Closing of the American Mind,* p. 382.

Index

Index